THE ESSENCE OF
T'AI CHI

Tao

Chi

WAYSUN LIAO

THE ESSENCE OF T'AI CHI

Illustrated by the author

SHAMBHALA
Boston & London
1995

Shambhala Publications, Inc.
Horticultural Hall
300 Massachusetts Avenue
Boston, Massachusetts 02115
http://www.shambhala.com

9 8 7 6 5 4 3

Printed in Singapore
⊗ This edition is printed on acid-free paper that
meets the American National Standards
Institute Z39.48 Standard.
Distributed in the United States by Random House, Inc.,
and in Canada by Random House of Canada Ltd

See page 163 for Library of Congress
Cataloging-in-Publication Data.

CONTENTS

CONTENTS

PREFACE

If you ask the question "How can I study T'ai Chi correctly?" those knowledgeable in this complicated, sophisticated, and sometimes mysterious field will probably smile and give you a less than satisfactory answer: "Go to a qualified teacher."

This answer will undoubtedly lead you to the next query: "What determines a qualified teacher, and are such people available?" The answer in this case is guaranteed to disappoint you: "Read a good T'ai Chi book."

Thoroughly frustrated by this time, you will probably ask, "Do I have to read every available T'ai Chi book in order to decide which contain authentic information and which instructors possess the proper background and abilities to qualify them in this discipline?" You most likely won't even get an answer to this question.

The above series of pertinent questions is commonly asked not only by Westerners, but by the Chinese themselves. Unfortunately, there is no clear-cut solution to the dilemma of the prospective student. There is only a limited selection of T'ai Chi books available, whether in English or in Chinese. Further, more often than not, the most famous instructors are not necessarily the most qualified, and a qualified master may not be in a position to teach his skills to others.

Traditionally, T'ai Chi instruction was carried out either in a temple or in the master's home, and training was conducted on a personal basis. The principles were transmitted mainly by word of mouth, rather than through the more permanent method of the written record. T'ai Chi was thus passed down verbally from generation to generation, more in the style of a folk art than as a structured system.

The few attempts that were made to commit T'ai Chi principles to writing were hampered by the limitations of a primitive printing process, which depended on the use of carved wooden blocks and presses. As this method was costly and time-consuming, articles to be published tended to be as condensed as possible. In addition, the language was often cryptic, and the use of one word for multiple meanings was common. Lastly, the tendency of T'ai Chi practitioners to monopolize instructional materials further reduced the availability of written texts.

As a result of these factors, there exist today only several brief pages of early manuscripts that stand as the authentic source for the correct study and practice of the art of T'ai Chi. These texts, which were written in a type of martial arts code, are known as *The T'ai Chi Classics I, II,* and *III* and are also commonly referred to as *The T'ai Chi Bible.*

Because of the T'ai Chi Classics' archaic language, complicated concepts, and use of certain technical terms and forms of sentence structure, the many attempts to translate them into modern English or Chinese have given rise to a great deal of controversy. The present book, rather than merely presenting yet another literal translation of the T'ai Chi Classics, has included in its pages precise explanations of such basic T'ai Chi principles as ch'i, jing, and internal energy cultivation. In this way, it is hoped that the student will develop a deeper, more complete understanding of both the philosophy of T'ai Chi and its application to the art. Also included are fresh translations of the three T'ai Chi Classics, with commentary on each aphorism. The actual forms of T'ai Chi Meditative Movement are illustrated in a number of different books on T'ai Chi, but the practice of T'ai Chi is best learned firsthand from a competent instructor. As an alternative, a video tape giving detailed instructions on the movements is available from:

The T'ai Chi Center
433 South Boulevard
Oak Park, IL 60302

It is hoped that the texts and the commentary presented here will serve as an inspiration for both beginning and advanced students of T'ai Chi.

EDITOR'S NOTE

The Essence of T'ai Chi is adapted from Waysun Liao's *T'ai Chi Classics* (Shambhala Publications, 1990) and includes the complete translations of *T'ai Chi Classics I, II,* and *III,* along with the complete text of Master Liao's commentary. Also included here are adapted versions of the preface, chapter 1, and chapter 2.

THE ESSENCE OF
T'AI CHI

"Eternal Energy"

1

HISTORICAL
AND
PHILOSOPHICAL
BACKGROUND

WHAT IS T'AI CHI?

T'ai Chi is a way of life that has been practiced by the Chinese for thousands of years.
We should look into three areas in order to
fully understand the historical background of
T'ai Chi: (1) its philosophical foundation,
(2) how it developed as a martial art, and (3)
how T'ai Chi instruction has been passed on
from generation to generation.

For those who are interested in the vivid,
rich heritage of Chinese culture, and especially those who wish to communicate with
and understand those persons from the
other side of the globe, it is necessary to
study the philosophy of T'ai Chi: that invisible, immense, and most powerful thought
that threads its way undiminished through
the entirety of oriental history. We are able
to do so thanks to a few good individuals
in each of countless generations who were
unselfishly dedicated to keeping the spirit of
T'ai Chi alive.

First, we may need to shed some of the beliefs and assumptions we have inherited. Human beings, knowing that they are not perfect, desire perfection and search for a better life. Historically, people have always made mistakes in this search because they have misunderstood the nature and potential of human life. Each generation has interpreted this potential differently; some have made religious assumptions while others have ignored or even denied the value of human life. As various social and organizational hierarchies develop and evolve into traditions, fundamental mistakes continue to be made. These accumulate and are often themselves perpetuated as tradition. If we naively follow our own tradition we may someday find out that we have made yet another mistake—the mistake of not questioning our traditions.

Even though our modern technology has brought us into the space age, the motivation of human life remains mysterious. Human achievements seem very small in the light of the historical progress of civilization. Yet even our theories of evolution are still in doubt; in spite of all our technology we still look up at the immense sky and wonder how it all started.

When we watch with pride and enjoyment the flight of a jumbo jet shrinking the earth beneath its wings, it is all too easy to forget that its flight is an imitation of the birds—merely the use of aerodynamic principles that were thousands of years old before humans first walked the earth. Our advanced medical technology has rocketed us to the super-sophisticated level of organ transplants, but we still have to succumb to the most basic and primitive needs: we must breathe air and eat food to survive.

We, the human inhabitants of this earth, may come to realize that fundamentally we have not progressed very far from the original inhabitants of this planet. We may come to see that we cannot change very much about ourselves.

A close look at our world's history reveals obvious cycles in which the development of the total person was either emphasized or ignored. When idealized human nature was emphasized, this yielded a very strong, creative civilization, one in which society progressed and people became spiritualized. Yet many mistakes still took place during this journey.

Several thousands of years ago, such idealism emerged in China. The Chinese of this period were searching for the highest form of life of the human mind and body. In their own unique manner, they achieved their goal—unlike Western civilizations, which separated body from mind and allowed spiritual development only in terms of religious, mystical ecstasy.

The Chinese conceived the human mind to be an unlimited dimension, but the scope of human activity to be moderate. The focus of their goal was a unified philosophy of human life and a simplification of beliefs. This was the birth of what we know today as T'ai Chi thought. T'ai Chi became the invisible power that guided the movements of Chinese history for thousands of years. It gave tremendous impetus to that fabulous culture, showing its influence in areas ranging from medicine to diet, from art to economics. Even the order of human relations was designed according to T'ai Chi ideals.

T'ai Chi means "the ultimate." It means improving, and progressing toward the unlimited; it means the immense existence and the great eternal. All of the various directions in which T'ai Chi influence was felt were guided by the theory of opposites: the *Yin* and the *Yang,* the negative and the positive. This is sometimes called the *original principle.* It was also believed that all of the various influences of T'ai Chi point in one direction: toward the ultimate.

According to T'ai Chi theory, the abilities

of the human body are capable of being developed beyond their commonly conceived potential. Civilization can be improved to the highest levels of achievement. Creativity has no boundaries whatsoever, and the human mind should have no restrictions or barriers placed upon its capabilities.

One reaches the ultimate level, or develops in that direction, by means of the ladder of balanced powers and their natural motions—Yin, the negative power (yielding), and Yang, the positive power (action). From the viewpoint of this theory, it is the interplay of constructive and destructive forces that causes the essence of life to materialize, the material world to manifest. And the spiraling movements of these forces seems endless.

That the two equal powers, Yin and Yang, oppose and yet complement each other has confused many throughout history. Explanations of the meaning of life have ranged from the theory that humans were born with sin already a part of their nature, through the hypothesis that it is not education but the fear of punishment that creates a good person, down to the view that if there were no civilization at all there would be no evil in the world.

The very fact that there is argument reveals the truth of the concept that two balanced powers exist. Our universe is programmed in such a way that the two powers exchange their essence, and existence comes from this. This natural law, obvious as it is, is ignored by most humans. We can easily rationalize our ignorance with the excuse that we ourselves are programmed to possess only one of the two powers—either male or female, for example.

This human tendency to ignore all other aspects and focus on only one side of an issue brought Western civilization into religious worship. Western religions did, as a matter of fact, stabilize civilization and the social order for thousands of years, but they also gave rise to a series of tragic and bloody wars between differing religious factions. Formal religions were often guilty of extreme and dogmatic attitudes. They sought to dominate by force rather than to promote harmony. They wielded influence so strong that humans could not easily shake it off, thus causing a wave of thought pollution whose effects still persist today.

In the sixteenth century, there were many free thinkers, such as Galileo, who tried to enlighten people, but religion held the reins. Talking and thinking were not enough; lifestyle changes were needed. So the cultural darkness of the Middle Ages was only finally broken by the Industrial Revolution, which in turn brought about dogmatism. This dogmatism is now being eclipsed by the free-minded, educated generations of today. The women's equal rights movement is an indication of the fact that women's power—the negative, the Yin—has been ignored, abused, deprived, oppressed, and misunderstood for centuries. The contributions of the negative power are as important as those of the positive power, just as the function of electricity consists of two opposite powers.

The Chinese have long realized that the two T'ai Chi elemental powers must interact, and the harmonious result could bring progress and unlimited development. Yet they have had no better luck at utilizing their knowledge than Westerners. While people in the West are freeing themselves from the shadows of religious idealism and creating the opportunity to experience the realities of the T'ai Chi principle, the Chinese have not yet been able to release themselves from the mental pollution of their own T'ai Chi–influenced culture.

About two thousand years ago in China, following the Spring and Autumn Age, the T'ai Chi principle began to be misused, or ignored. There then followed several hundred years of Dark Ages, during which time the development of human relations and political power took place in a very inferior fashion.

T'ai Chi encourages the fulfillment of the individual person, yet also emphasizes that this goal should be achieved through moderate, natural ways of living. Examination of Chinese history shows that at a certain point this idea began to be applied only in terms of political power struggles: to be the ultimate person was to be the most powerful ruler. The idea of a simple, natural human nature was ignored.

The Ch'ing Dynasty cast the mold of authoritarian control and slavery that was to become the tradition throughout ensuing Chinese history. To the rulers—the Yang, aggressive powers—went the benefits, the ultimate power; while those who were yielding, cooperative, obedient, and who encouraged harmony—those possessing the Yin power—were forced to become the subjects. Women were educated to be weak and helpless, the designated slaves, and men were trained to be followers of the ultimate power who was, of course, the king. To become the ultimate power oneself, one merely had to resort to the use of violence—extreme Yang power. Competitiveness and aggressiveness were encouraged but moderated, all for the benefit of the rulers. Ironically, it was this social tradition that carried on the T'ai Chi principle for hundreds of years. As a consequence, even though T'ai Chi was discovered and initiated in China so early, it followed the same sad destiny as did Western philosophy.

Whereas religion was to become the core of Western civilization, it was either ignored or abused in China. Although the Buddhist religion was imported from India and then absorbed by the Chinese culture, its spiritual philosophy was de-emphasized, while its ceremonies and rites became fashionable. In Chinese Buddhism, the ideal of self-control was emphasized. The emperor used this ideal to suppress the common people, so that religion became known as "the ruler's favorite tool." T'ai Chi philosophy, however, offered beliefs that fulfilled human needs, even though its ideals were also abused by generations of the powerful and greedy.

For the Chinese, who have received all of the influence of T'ai Chi culture but also, sadly, all of the pollution of a social system abused by power, there is much to be learned from Western culture. Westerners have already been released from the bondage of religious influence yet are still trying to put their ideals into actuality. Really, all people search for the ultimate today; we seek a peaceful way, a natural way, a way to motivate our civilization toward the ultimate. Coincidentally, our ideals perfectly match those of the T'ai Chi way.

Hundreds of years ago, those who searched for a way to elevate the human body and spirit to their ultimate level developed an ingenious system known as the T'ai Chi Exercise. This system, which was inspired by the T'ai Chi outlook and which was based on principles not clearly known or understood by its founders, has since proved to be the most advanced system of body exercise and mind conditioning ever to be created.

While the Chinese ruling class was interested only in T'ai Chi's productive benefits, those who cared nothing about authority were adapting the philosophy to their personal lifestyles. They were applying the idea of a natural harmony to the development of the body and mind. Since this was of relatively little interest to the rulers, there is no real historical evidence of just when T'ai Chi as a mind and body system actually began.

All of the traditional Chinese arts, such as brush painting, calligraphy, literature, poetry, and cooking, emphasized the Yin/Yang principle as the means of reaching the ultimate. The complete philosophy of T'ai Chi therefore became an integral aspect of these arts. However, the T'ai Chi system of mind and body discipline was unique in that it explicitly applied the original T'ai Chi principles in a progressive, organized manner. Therefore, it has become the only complete system to preserve this great philosophy for hundreds of years—all the way down to today's complicated world.

THE SYSTEMATIZATION OF T'AI CHI

For thousands of years, the system of political rule in China was based on brutality and corruption. Those who were dedicated to the truth called themselves Taoists or "mountain men," and they lived a life similar to that of the monk. They carried on the spirit of T'ai Chi philosophy and in no way interfered with the ruling authorities. Since T'ai Chi formed its own independent system and had nothing to do with political structures, it was able to enjoy growth and freedom of development, even if only in small, isolated communities of dedicated men.

While these groups had no ties with the governing authorities, their studies were nonetheless respected by the rulers, first as a body of accumulated knowledge and later as a form of religion. Gradually T'ai Chi came to be considered a highly advanced form of folk art, to be studied exclusively by intellectuals and to be passed on from generation to generation.

Approximately 1700 years ago, a famous Chinese medical doctor, Hua-Tuo, emphasized physical and mental exercise as a means of improving health. He believed that human beings should exercise and imitate the movements of animals, such as birds, tigers, snakes, and bears, to recover original life abilities that had been lost. He therefore organized the folk fighting arts into a fighting art called the Five Animals Games. This was the first systematized martial art in China. Since then, the Five Animal Games have been popular with the Chinese, who practice them for health and exercise.

Around 475 C.E., Ta-Mo (Bodhidharma) came to China from India to spread his religious teachings, and he resided in the Shaolin Temple in the Tang Fung area of North China. Besides religious worship and meditation, he included physical training in the daily routine. He used the Five Animal Games to develop in his followers a balanced mental and physical discipline. Dedication toward Buddhism, combined with an abundance of time for practice, allowed the Five Animal Games to develop in this context to a very high level of achievement as a martial art.

When the followers of Ta-Mo spread their religious beliefs throughout China they also carried with them their martial art achievement. The system developed by the monks from the Shaolin Temple came to be known as the Shaolin martial art system. It emphasized physical toughening and strengthening, as well as spiritual development. This was the dawn of the systematic development of the *external* martial arts in China.

The mental discipline aspect of the Shaolin system was based mainly on Buddhist meditation. To those Chinese steeped in sophisticated Taoism and Yin/Yang philosophy, it was, and is still, considered to be simply a physical fighting system.

In 1200 C.E., the Taoist monk Chang San-feng founded a temple in Wu-tang Mountain for the practice of Taoism, for the ultimate development of human life. Master Chang emphasized Yin/Yang harmony as a means to advance the development of mental and physical ability, natural meditation, as well as natural body movements propelled by an internal energy which would be developed at a certain level of achievement.

Since the Shaolin system had already been spreading throughout China for hundreds of years, the idea of adapting Taoist theory to everyday life instead of making it into a form of religious worship was readily accepted by Chinese society. T'ai Chi thought and its Yin/Yang philosophy soon developed as a temple-style organization based on the model of the Shaolin Temple. A modified form of monastic training was adopted in order to promote the sophisticated system in missionary fashion.

From its inception, the temple system at Wu-tang Mountain emphasized internal power and the development of wisdom. Thus, the Chinese have commonly referred to the T'ai Chi system as the *internal* system, to distinguish it from the Shaolin fighting art system.

Through the years, there have also been systems that combine elements of both the T'ai Chi and Shaolin arts into moderately developed martial arts. These are known today as *Hsing-I,* the Form and Mind system, and *Pakua,* the Eight Diagram martial art system.

Since a great deal of effort and concentration, as well as firm dedication, were required in order to reach even a fair level of achievement in T'ai Chi, a monastic system soon developed, and enrollment became an exclusive privilege. Those who reached high degrees of achievement became the leaders of the system, and, followed by their enthusiasts, they evolved a unique training relationship between master and disciple.

This tradition played an important role in passing on T'ai Chi knowledge and wisdom to society, and the immense power of its influence was able to pour deeply into all social classes. Supported by the common people, and at times even by the emperors (as when Master Chang San-feng was summoned to advise the rulers on Taoist philosophy), the temple-style T'ai Chi system shaped the strong image that T'ai Chi was the ultimate art of life. Masters of T'ai Chi were regarded as the symbol of wisdom. They received great respect, especially since they practiced justice, charity, education, and the medicinal arts as part of their lifestyle.

Those who practiced T'ai Chi at times played a role in the enforcement of China's codes of human morality. For hundreds of years, the Chinese depended on only these codes as the law of the land. They were obeyed by everyone, even the emperors, and they were the foundation of the peace and social order of the Chinese civilization. Rules of basic human conduct—kindness, respect for one's elders, fidelity to parents, and love of one's kin—were enforced as strictly as written laws. Whereas the laws of today's industrial society say nothing, for example, about the immorality of deserting an elderly and needy parent, in the Chinese society of several hundred years ago such an act would have been considered a serious offense and would have been severely punished.

Followers of T'ai Chi believed that people should discipline themselves to be spiritual, healthy, kind, and intelligent; to be responsible for assisting others to reach the same levels of achievement; to enjoy the truth; to fight fearlessly against immorality and injustice; and to protect the needy and the weak. It was with these goals in mind that the martial art aspect of T'ai Chi came to be developed and emphasized.

T'ai Chi theories were easily applied to the martial arts. Mind and body harmony, in tune with the natural order of things, was at the core of T'ai Chi. This offered a direction of development completely different from that of other forms of fighting techniques. It also yielded awesome results in terms of human abilities coming from the power of the mind. Thus T'ai Chi Ch'uan became the most powerful martial art ever known.

Throughout Chinese history, periods of unrest always led to local power formations and the use of force. In some cases, even T'ai Chi practitioners became involved in the enforcement of peace in their areas, with the result that instruction in the martial art aspect of T'ai Chi was urgently needed. The philosophical and meditation aspects of the art were gradually ignored by most people, with instruction in T'ai Chi becoming almost completely limited to its martial art aspect.

The true, dedicated masters of T'ai Chi remained in the mountains, and, along with their followers, they led a monastic life in order to carry on the pure art. They meditated and practiced daily in order to attune the spirit, condition the mind, discipline the body, and elevate the essence. In this way the original system was preserved more or less intact, with both mind and body discipline still being included in the training.

During the times when peace was re-established and the need for self-defense training faded away, those who had taught the art professionally carried on their dedicated careers as a type of family business. They taught only those who were most seriously interested, especially any of their own children who wanted to study the art as their profession. Herbal medicine and acupuncture were also offered to the local community on a charitable basis. Financial support depended on contributions by the local people whom they served, and by their students.

Family surnames came to be associated with the different styles of T'ai Chi that were being passed on, mouth to ear, from generation to generation—for example, the Ch'en style, the Yang style, and the Wu style. Many of these are still known today. Each style was distinctive, but all followed the classic T'ai Chi principles. Today, temple-style T'ai Chi is still considered the most authentic system, but since the rapid changes of industrial society allow little space for such a sophisticated system to grow, it has declined and is disappearing. Family-style T'ai Chi is also diminishing.

About 350 years ago, in 1644 C.E., the Manchurians invaded the Chinese empire and established the Ch'ing Dynasty. Although the dynasty was founded by force and for the benefit of the rulers, the Manchus were soon absorbed into the Chinese culture. They adopted a Chinese lifestyle, reconstructed a peaceful order of society, and started a period of corrupt rule that was to last for centuries.

In the early stages of the dynasty, episodes of hostility and conflict between the Chinese and their Manchurian rulers were serious and often brutal. Even though the Manchus tried very hard to learn the culture and adapt themselves to the Chinese ways, native Chinese still regarded them as barbarians. The people's feelings of responsibility toward their nation diminished; passive resistance and refusal to cooperate with the "outsiders" resulted in the stagnation of the country's economic development.

As soon as the Ch'ing empire builders heard about the sophisticated art of T'ai Chi, they drafted the most famous master of the times, Yang Lu-chang (1799–1872), founder of the Yang style or Yang family system, into royal service. Unwilling to teach the Manchus, Master Yang deliberately modified the

T'ai Chi meditation forms, converting them into a kind of slow-moving, outer exercise and completely ignoring the inner philosophy and mental disciple which is the key to T'ai Chi.

Master Yang knew that if the royal family learned of his unwillingness to teach them, and of his modifications, the emperor would take retribution for this offense and appease his anger by murdering not only him, but his entire family. Since Master Yang felt he could trust no one except his own sons, it was to them and to no one else that he taught the genuine art of T'ai Chi. In this way he avoided implicating anyone else in his personal decision to deceive the royalty.

From that time on, the family style of T'ai Chi became more restricted, with masters teaching the art only to their own kin. It was said that some masters would not even dare to teach the art to their daughters; when the girl married, a new relative could be linked with the Imperial Family, or could be someone whom the master felt should not be allowed into the art.

While the family style of T'ai Chi decreased, the exercise style was encouraged and practiced by members of the Imperial Family. It soon became the fad of the leisure class throughout China, and it remained so until the end of the Ch'ing Dynasty.

When the revolution of 1900–1910 succeeded in overthrowing the corrupt rulers, the noble families, deprived of their power, scattered throughout the country. T'ai Chi, of course, traveled with them. Practitioners claimed the authenticity of their art, stating that it had been taught to them by masters of the Yang family, or of other T'ai Chi families, and the public naturally accepted their claims.

In this way, the modified form of T'ai Chi became today's T'ai Chi Ch'uan, or the so-called T'ai Chi Exercise. This is the T'ai Chi practiced publicly in China today; it is the T'ai Chi Dance, also called the Chinese Ballet by some Westerners. In these modern times, a person may receive instruction in and practice the art of T'ai Chi for years, and, regardless of which style is being taught, still stand a very good chance of learning only "public T'ai Chi." In other words, most of the T'ai Chi practiced today is not the original T'ai Chi, and it is devoid of meaning.

However, Master Yang Lu-chan's forced instruction did serve a useful purpose. Although public T'ai Chi is merely a shadow of the original, classical, temple-style T'ai Chi, it offers the greatest opportunity for the Chinese people and for others of the world to be introduced to the art. As a matter of fact, if the Ch'ing Dynasty's rulers had not become interested in T'ai Chi, it might have disappeared altogether under the rising tide of industrialization.

It is when a person becomes serious in the study of T'ai Chi that the search for the authentic art, the temple style, begins. One can only then appreciate the courage and dedication of the masters who have preserved the line of temple T'ai Chi down through the centuries. This is our heritage.

大道千秋

正氣浩然

*"The eternal energy
is all-powerful and omnipresent.
The eternal Tao is everlasting."*

2

CH'I

*The Internal Energy
of T'ai Chi*

Thousands of years ago, Chinese Taoists, whether from scientific observation, by mere hypothesis, or by obtaining information from sources unknown to us today, formulated the theory that there is an eternal power that moves the universe. They called this ultimate power *ch'i*. According to the legendary theory of Yin and Yang, ch'i exercises its powers ceaselessly, moving in a balanced manner between the positive (constructive) and negative (destructive) powers.

Because the Yin and Yang powers originate from the ultimate power, ch'i, they are able to move freely without any external limitation, immune from the restrictions of space, time, and even the material manifestations of existence. Because the two powers are always conflicting yet balancing each other, our universe is constantly and indefinitely changing. Everything, even unfilled space, derives its existence from the balanced interaction of these two contrasting forces. Since the powers of Yin and Yang are the origin of everything, they are the ultimate nature of every object in this universe.

The human being, also a part of the universe, is powered by the same source of energy—ch'i. The process of human life is based on the interaction of Yin and Yang forces. Our life increases and changes, and for reasons that are still mysterious to us, it follows a natural cycle and eventually dies. Ancient Chinese explain this cycle as the growth and fading of ch'i. It is ch'i that determines human mental and physical conditions. The way in which ch'i is expressed is commonly known as the *nature* of things.

It is the development of ch'i in the human body, along with the theory of the contrasting powers of Yin and Yang, that makes the art of T'ai Chi such a unique mental and physical system of discipline. Without correct training, or at least a full and clear understanding of the concept of ch'i, the true meaning of T'ai Chi will be lost. A simple analogy should help to explain this: ch'i is to

T'ai Chi what gasoline is to a gas-powered engine. Just as without gasoline the engine could not have been invented, if there had been no concept of ch'i development, the art of T'ai Chi would never have come to be.

In order to be able to practice T'ai Chi in the correct manner and thus receive the true benefit of the art, there are several terms that should first be fully understood.

Ch'i. The Chinese word *ch'i* literally means "air," "power," "motion," "energy," or "life." According to T'ai Chi theory, the correct meaning of *ch'i* is "intrinsic energy," "internal energy," or "original, eternal, and ultimate energy." The way in which ch'i expresses itself, going always to the nearest position of balance and harmony, is called *T'ai Chi*—"the grand ultimate."

Yin Ch'i or Yang Ch'i. Ch'i that is in a process of changing from one formation to another, or from one self-balancing situation to another, is termed either *Yin ch'i* or *Yang ch'i.*

Shen. T'ai Chi is based on the principle of three levels of energy. The base level, the essence or life energy, is inherent in the living organism. The next stage or level, ch'i, is a higher-than-normal manifestation of life energy. It supports the essence and is related to the function of mind. When ch'i is purified it elevates to the third stage: *shen,* or spirit. Shen is a much higher form of energy than ch'i and feels very different from ch'i.

Jing or Nei Jing. The power that is generated by ch'i is called *jing,* commonly known as *nei jing,* the internal power. In our analogy of the gasoline engine, jing would be equivalent to the horsepower generated by the gasoline's energy. If a person studies T'ai Chi for a number of years, he may generate a considerable amount of ch'i but may not necessarily be able to convert this ch'i into internal power, jing. Experientially, you can only feel another person's jing and not his ch'i; but you can only feel your own ch'i and not your jing. When practicing T'ai Chi as a

martial art, you utilize your ch'i by projecting jing directly into your opponent.

Jing operates outside the parameters of
space and time. Initially one uses imaging
power, or imagination, to identify and direct
the energy flow in the body, and then one
accelerates it. These theories, or principles,
are on the horizon of today's physical and
medical sciences. In the medical field, treat-
ments are already being used that have the
patient imagine or visualize his immune system moving to search out cancer cells and
destroy them. Success varies according to
each individual's power and control of his
imagination.

Li. The physical strength resulting from
body movement is called *li,* the physical
force. A simple way to describe the differ-
ence between li and jing is to say that li requires direct physical motion whereas jing
comes only from indirect motion. If you
bring your hand back and throw a punch forward, the result of the accumulated physical

energy is called li. If no drawing-back motion is required, and yet power can be transferred with the same effect, then jing, the vibration power of converted ch'i, has been applied. Whereas ch'i is controlled by the mind, li is operated by the physical mechanism.

HOW TO CULTIVATE CH'I

Everyone possesses ch'i and has possessed it since birth. Ch'i remains with the individual throughout life, dispersing only after death. There are two main steps involved in cultivating ch'i within your body: meditation and movement.

Meditation

In T'ai Chi practice, meditation is the only way to become aware of one's ch'i. After assuming either a simple sitting posture or an upright stance, the beginner can easily achieve success in T'ai Chi meditation by following these procedures:

1. Relax the entire body, as if you were asleep, making sure that there is no physical tension at all.
2. Calm your mind and concentrate on the total body, listening to its breath, sensing its pulse, and so on, until you can feel the body's natural rhythm.
3. Bring up your spirit by pushing up your crown point. Imagine an invisible string pulling your crown point from above. Gradually apply deeper breathing and inhale directly into the *tan t'ien* (an area located approximately three inches below the navel and two and one-half inches inward).

After weeks or months of practice, you may start to sense a feeling that flows with the rhythm of deep meditation breathing. This is ch'i, the internal energy. As you progress, this feeling grows stronger, and you can begin to sense and control the flow of this energy without the assistance of deep breathing. At this stage, you can use your mind to guide your chi's path of travel inside your body.

T'ai Chi Meditative Movement

After you are able to sense the flow of your chi, you can begin to practice the T'ai Chi Form in a meditative manner, allowing your chi to flow in accordance with your mind and body. With repeated practice, the sense of chi gradually increases. Your form also improves, becoming more graceful and harmonious and developing into a natural state which cannot be achieved by merely copying an instructor's form.

At this stage, your mind can guide your ch'i; it flows freely, directing your body and its movements at will. In this way your mind and body will reach harmony. If you wish to develop a strong internal energy, then you should practice the T'ai Chi Meditative Movement intensively. Exercising in the T'ai Chi manner is the only way to eventually generate immense internal energy and allow it to flow.

Many practitioners of T'ai Chi who claim to have been in the art for years still have developed no feeling of ch'i. This is because they neither practice correctly nor combine any meditative techniques with the T'ai Chi movements.

CONDENSING BREATHING: THE PROCESS THAT TURNS CH'I INTO JING

Once you are able to feel the intrinsic energy flowing freely throughout the body, you can introduce these feelings into each meditative movement in order to cultivate your ch'i, so that it grows stronger within you. However, without any further training process, the ch'i will remain within the body and will offer no greater benefits than a heightened awareness of your own body.

To further utilize ch'i it is necessary to practice a more advanced T'ai Chi meditation technique: *condensing breathing*. When you utilize this process, your internal energy will be generated into internal power, and this will be beneficial in many areas of your life.

Recalling the previous analogy of the gasoline engine, in order to generate horsepower, it is necessary to have a process that will burn the gasoline and so convert the fuel into a different, more functional form of power. Similarly, unless you "burn" your internal energy (ch'i) you cannot generate internal power (jing). The student must therefore take several steps to achieve this transformation. This process, known as T'ai Chi condensing breathing, is described below.

How to Practice Condensing Breathing

1. Preparation

In a stance that is somewhere between preparation and beginning form, relax your entire body, calm the mind, and gradually begin to do T'ai Chi meditation.

The eyes look into infinity, the crown point is pushed up and suspended, ears are listening inward, the tongue is rolled toward the back of the mouth with the teeth and lips lightly touching together, the ch'i is concentrated downward into the tan t'ien and flows smoothly, circulating throughout the body. Breathing is long, slow, smooth, rhythmic, and continuous.

2. Procedure

After experiencing the free flow of ch'i within your body, begin to pay extra attention to both of your arms. Try to sense and locate the bone structure while ignoring the existence of the surrounding muscles. In other words, imagine that only the skeleton is suspended there. As you inhale, imagine that your breath forces the bone to condense inward toward the bone marrow, as if the bone structure itself were being condensed and shrunk each time you inhaled. Repeat this exercise many times, and you will experience unusual feelings around your arms, such as cold, tingling, trembling, heat, or other sensations that will vary according to the individual.

3. Expanding Your Practice

After successfully practicing condensing breathing in both arms, apply the same technique to other areas of the body: spinal column, head, legs, and so on. For example, concentrate on the spinal column, imagining that it is absolutely erect, and try to use your feeling to locate first the total column and then each individual vertebra. Practice the condensing technique until you start to get a substantial feeling of the result.

Some areas may appear to be more sensitive to this type of practice, yielding feelings much faster than others. For example, the collar bone can be very slow in showing positive results. But consistent, faithful practice will eventually lead to success. You will need to consult with a qualified instructor in order to differentiate between genuine feelings and imagination.

It is recommended that the student follow the proper sequence of practice: hands, arms, spinal column, head, legs, and finally all the remaining parts of the body. Generally, a beginner can start to feel the transformation of ch'i into jing (a sensation similar to an electric shock) within several months.

Generating Jing from Ch'i

After the above steps have been practiced over a reasonable period of time, you can begin to experience authentic T'ai Chi working internally, generating the original life energy, ch'i, into the high-frequency vibration power, jing. This is what makes T'ai Chi, as, its name suggests, the grand ultimate art. You should now practice as follows.

First, stand with a relaxed and natural posture in a stance that is somewhere between beginning and preparation. Be sure to bear all of the important T'ai Chi principles in mind: upward suspension of the crown point; listening inwardly; eyes looking to infinity; breathing through the nose with a slow, smooth, continuous rhythm; tongue rolled upward, toward the back of the mouth; ch'i sunk downward to the tan t'ien; and so forth.

Slowly raise both hands as you inhale; meditate while applying the principles of

condensing breathing to the entire body. You should feel that the skeletal structure is suspended, without any muscles holding it. As you inhale and meditate, contract and squeeze the muscles around the bones toward the bone marrow. Relax the whole body as you exhale.

You should feel as if you are gathering all the energy of the body into the bone marrow on each inhale, and then relaxing yourself totally with each exhale. Repeat this exercise as often as possible, but stop immediately if your concentration weakens or fatigue occurs.

In this process you should treat the entire body and mind as one integrated unit. Use your mind to control the feeling of the ch'i and then "squeeze" the ch'i into the very center of the bone marrow each time you inhale. This will finally yield a trembling feeling similar to that caused by an electric shock. In later stages of practice, this sensation will get stronger and the feelings become more substantial, clearly separating themselves from imagination.

Ch'i flows through the body constantly.

As you use your mind to squeeze the ch'i toward your bone marrow, a strong wave-like current of energy similar to electricity is produced. The vibrations of this current are accelerated drastically during the periods when the work of squeezing persists.

In the advanced stages of this type of practice, you can accumulate the kind of feelings that will allow you to guide the direction in which the ch'i flows and circulates. As ch'i flows along the path down which you have sent it, it feels as if an electric current is flowing as a wave from one area to another. This current eventually becomes so strong that it yields a tremendous amount of vibration, accumulating in wave after wave and at a speed that only the mind is capable of generating. This creates the awesome power known as jing.

When someone is generating his jing and transmitting it to an area of his body, another person can sense the vibrations through mere physical contact. When two people are simultaneously experiencing jing within their bodies, they become more sensitive to the jing in each other. Martial artists of ancient China claimed they could judge how good another martial artist's fighting ability was by mere feeling or sensation. They were able to gauge another's skill by the amount and speed of their internal power, rather than by assessing their physical condition.

Once again using the analogy of the gasoline engine, the size of the engine does not necessarily determine the horsepower that it produces.

What makes the practice of T'ai Chi the "grand ultimate" of all the arts is the *internal work* involved. Internal work (*nei kong*) means the use of internal exercises to bring total control, harmony, and awareness to the mind and body. As discussed earlier, after rousing the awareness of ch'i within your body, you transform this energy into jing, the substantial power, by the condensing breathing exercise. Jing can be recycled when it is not transmitted or used. This means that you can guide the vibrations of jing to cause your ch'i to move vigorously within your body and so strengthen your ch'i, the vital energy of life. In turn, the stronger the flow of ch'i, the greater the amount of jing that can be produced.

HOW TO INCREASE CH'I AWARENESS

Ch'i is the origin of our life energy; in other words, our life is determined by ch'i. Consequently, a stronger flow of ch'i will ensure stronger life energy. Chinese tradition holds that ch'i flows ceaselessly in the human body. Whenever there is an interference of the flow, or the path is blocked, sickness occurs.

Chinese doctors have always strongly believed that cultivating and strengthening the body's ch'i can cure disease and correct malfunctions of every kind. Such concepts present a complex puzzle to even the most pioneering of Western scientists, who are at a loss to come up with a testing device that would either verify or disprove the existence of ch'i.

This lack of empirical proof has given rise to many debates between those who would embrace the concept of ch'i and those who would insist that it cannot possibly exist. Those who insist that there is no ch'i base their view on today's scientific knowledge, especially that of anatomy, electronics, and chemical analysis. Their argument is that if ch'i cannot be demonstrated then it must not exist. The exponents of ch'i, however, say that if it does not exist, why has it dominated the philosophy of Chinese medicine and the practice of T'ai Chi for so many centuries?

Ch'i is not an element of any kind, but rather it is the origin of everything. Ch'i does not even create itself because, being immune to the laws of creation and destruction, it merely continues to exist. Those who would deny the existence of ch'i, therefore, find that no matter what their arguments are, their understanding of ch'i is far distant from its true meaning.

Setting aside all arguments and opinions about the existence or nonexistence of ch'i, let us examine this phenomenon, with the hope of providing some clues that will help us better understand it. Since ch'i is not an element of matter, it cannot be directly examined by any instrument at this time. Since it is the ultimate energy from which the entire universe and the essence of all existence is derived, ch'i is even immune to the limitations of time and space. This means that because there is ch'i, so there is space. From the T'ai Chi viewpoint, space is not merely emptiness nor just an imaginary concept; rather it is something that is formed by, and subsequently filled with, ch'i.

The assumption that there is an ultimate formation of energy which is beyond the conventional interpretations of existence, and which can thus escape the limitations of time and space, would seem to be self-contradictory and so unacceptable to human reason. Yet this assumption is the foundation of T'ai Chi, the beginning force of Taoism, and the cornerstone of the Chinese cultural pattern.

Skepticism about the existence of ch'i can easily lead to the rationalization that ch'i is a product of the imagination. For example, many people try to explain ch'i as a miracle, as the result of a religious belief of the kind usually associated with some form of church worship. This attitude is of course an over-simplification. For if ch'i were merely the result of faith and human belief, then it would of necessity disappear if one did not believe in it. The feeling of ch'i circulating within the body can be felt, however, whether or not one has a fertile imagination. In contrast, no matter how hard you try, imagining that you are growing a pair of horns on your head won't cause you to wake up one day to find them substantially manifested for all the world to see. Placing ch'i in the realm of the imagination is thus merely another futile attempt to rationalize it out of existence.

Although in the beginning a certain amount of imagination is needed in order to sharpen your awareness of your own internal energy, the feeling of ch'i flow will, with consistent practice, become substantial enough to convince you that the force flowing within you is real, and not just the product of an overactive imagination.

Since ch'i is what forms our life energy, it follows that everyone has ch'i. But before you try to discipline your ch'i, you must first become aware of its flow within the body. A simple analogy may clarify this: gasoline is produced by refining oil, an element that occurs naturally underground. Before gasoline can be obtained, the oil must first be located, collected from its natural source, and put through the refining process. In the same way, the body already has ch'i; you do not produce it. It is, however, up to you to accumulate your ch'i, reorganize it, and use it to generate the internal power, jing.

The T'ai Chi practitioner can increase the awareness of ch'i by means of the following steps:

1. Relaxation practice
2. Breath control
3. Concentration development
4. Coordination practice
5. Meditation and imagination
6. T'ai Chi meditative movement practice
7. Two-person practice
8. Auxiliary training

By following these steps, which are described in detail in the following pages, the T'ai Chi practitioner, whether beginning or

advanced, will gain increased awareness of
the ch'i within.

Relaxation Practice:
Shoong

Shoong means "to relax," "to lose," "to give
up," "to yield." It is a term that has been
adapted and incorporated into the special-
ized terminology traditionally used by T'ai
Chi masters. It is said that when the famous
T'ai Chi master Yang Chen-fu was training
the late master Cheng Man-ch'ing, Master
Yang reminded his student daily to "be
shoong, be really, really shoong." "If you are
not shoong," Master Yang would say, "even
just a little bit not shoong, you are not in the
stage of shoong. You are then in the stage of
a loser of T'ai Chi; you will be defeated."

Since T'ai Chi masters have always emphasized relaxation, shoong has been a sub-
ject of interest to T'ai Chi practitioners for
centuries. Many have tried to interpret the

true meaning of shoong. Indeed, many explanations of what shoong really is have been offered, but little effort has been made to define it authentically, in the classical way. As a result, T'ai Chi students have frequently been misled.

Years ago, as I chatted and had tea with Master Cheng Man-ch'ing in his attic study (a room he had named the Long Evening Library), he pointed out that, as babies, human beings are relaxed and totally yielding. But after they grow and become "civilized," they are no longer shoong at all. I was shocked by his words, for they showed that, after having taught T'ai Chi for almost half a century, Master Cheng was feeling frustrated by his teaching experiences.

Master Cheng asked me how I would explain the true meaning of relaxation to my own students in the Chicago area. I told him that I had to use a great many analogies to describe it. I then asked him about his own method of explaining shoong. "Are you still telling your advanced students that you once dreamed that you lost both arms and since then you have realized the true meaning of shoong?" I asked jokingly. We both laughed. Master Cheng used to tell his students that after he had had that dream his T'ai Chi practice had improved and his ch'i flowed smoothly.

Master Cheng's dream, described partly in seriousness and partly in jest, does help to explain the true meaning of relaxation. Because we use our hands to do most of our work, they are the main source of tension in our body. A beginning T'ai Chi practitioner uses only his hands to perform the movements, without involving the rest of his body. This is why the body appears so stiff. How can a person truly relax if his body is stiff?

In T'ai Chi meditative movement practice, relaxation means to give yourself up completely, both mentally and physically. It means to yield: yield totally to the entire universe, yield to the infinite. When you are able to yield yourself totally to the infinite, you will be able to relax and merge into the unity which the Taoist philosophy describes as the "integration of sky and human."

In other words, if you remain yourself, you will be excluded from the totality of the universe. If, however, you can give up yourself, then you will truly become part of the universe.

When a cup of water is placed on the surface of a lake, the water is not lake water because it is held away from the larger body by the rigid walls of its container, and so it is unable to yield to the greater force. So, using your imagination, feel that you are as pliable as water, totally flexible, yielding to the shape of the container. When the water that is you is poured into the lake, you are the lake.

If the analogy of the water doesn't work for you, another approach is to meditate that you are floating in the air. As you float, allow your body to become transparent so that the air can circulate through.

The T'ai Chi practitioner should do a great deal of meditation to relax body and mind, in order to be able to combine with the universe. When you achieve this level, you will flow as the universe flows, move as the universe moves. It is then that you will really appreciate the true meaning of shoong in T'ai Chi.

As Master Yang reminded his students constantly, "*Relax; relax completely, as if the body is transparent.*" And Master Cheng advised, "Relax; each joint, each part of your body should open up and be loose." Unless you reach a state of total mental and physical relaxation (shoong), the flow of ch'i cannot be felt. Therefore, the T'ai Chi practitioner should spend a great deal of time meditating in order to gain awareness of ch'i.

Mental relaxation is much more important than physical relaxation, because mental tension will undoubtedly cause physical stiffness. Beginners should start with a calmed mind, progress to a totally relaxed body, and then meditate with the universe. This will allow the practitioner to sense the rhythmic power waves of the universe and to eventually increase the awareness of the ch'i circulation within the body, as if it circulated with the entire universe.

Breath Control

In ancient China, T'ai Chi followers and Taoists adopted breathing techniques to increase the awareness of ch'i. Hence, in the Chinese language *ch'i* and *air* share the same word. In general, the feeling ch'i flow within the body is guided by and results from the feeling of deep breathing.

In the beginning stages of awareness, ch'i feels like the inhaled air flowing through the body. Gradually one can sense that, throughout the entire body, ch'i circulates with the air. The beginner who is eager for the feeling of ch'i should take the following steps in his or her practice.

1. Preparation

Observe all of the basic T'ai Chi principles, such as upward suspension of the crown point, neck relaxed while the head is kept vertical, tongue rolled upward and backward, teeth and lips closed, and the entire body relaxed. Practice can be done in a sitting or standing posture or, if possible, in the T'ai Chi stance.

2. Nose to Tan T'ien Path

After making sure that you are completely relaxed, loosen your belt and concentrate on your stomach. When you inhale through your nostrils, control your breath, making it long, thin, and continuous. Slowly guide the breath and press it downward toward the area of the lower stomach. The stomach expands, inflating as the air is brought into it.

Wait for a moment, until you feel that there is a need to exhale, and then slowly contract your stomach muscles and push the air upward and out through your nose.

After completing the exhalation, repeat the process many times. Each time you inhale, imagine that the air is being driven all the way to the tan t'ien, and then back upward when you exhale. Be careful not to force your breathing to the extreme, or past the point of discomfort. Always practice in a moderate manner.

Anatomically, the process is simply one of inhaling a large volume of air into the lungs and forcing it to press the diaphragm downward. It then moves upward on the exhale. It is claimed by most Chinese doctors that such an exercise can regulate blood circulation, especially to the lower internal organs (liver, kidneys, and spleen). They also claim that it can regulate heart functions, because the exercise that the diaphragm receives stimulates the vital nerve center of the lower spinal column.

This type of breathing practice also increases the secretion of saliva and calms the nerves. Nevertheless, despite all the benefits involved, the main purpose of the process is to develop, through proper control of the breathing process, a feeling of the rhythm of the body and a harmony of the mind.

3. Turning the T'ai Chi Ball

Another practice in the T'ai Chi breath-control process, known as Turning the T'ai Chi Ball, can be used to increase breath control and consequently increase the awareness of the ch'i feeling. In this practice we consider the lower abdominal area as assuming the shape of a round ball during the inhalation process.

After you achieve success in the Nose to Tan T'ien Path practice, further control can be achieved by bringing the tender musculature at the *fei-yin* (the area defined by the *M. pectinius* muscle in the front and *M. gracilius* in the back) upward and backward toward the base of the spine.

As you inhale, exert only enough pressure to form the tan t'ien area into a round ball. It will automatically tend to turn backward and upward. Beginners will start to sense the tan t'ien area turning after several weeks of concentrated practice. More advanced students will sense an increased number of turns before each exhale and will soon feel the turbine-like spin of their ch'i as soon as the fei-yin muscles are brought up with the inhale.

It is recommended that this type of practice be done in a cautious manner and only after consulting with a highly qualified instructor. It has been reported that improper practice methods have caused overanxious students certain physical malfunctions, such as gastric disorders, stomach problems, hemorrhoids, and so on.

4. Tan T'ien through the Spinal Column Path

After successful practice of the preceding steps, you can proceed to guide the feeling of ch'i upward along the spinal column, starting from the base of the spine, all the way to a point directly between the shoulder blades. On the exhale, the ch'i is guided along the shoulders and down the arms to the center of the palms, as well as from the tan t'ien to the spinal column, to the nostrils, and out of the body. The ch'i should be directed along both paths at the same time, on the exhale.

When a beginner experiences difficulty in sensing the ch'i flowing upward along the spinal column, he may build up the feeling by simply pulling both shoulders forward slightly and extending and crossing both arms in front of the chest. This provides a guide to building up the feeling of ch'i flow. Eventually the ch'i flow will be sensed without the assistance of this temporary maneuver.

5. *Spinal Column to Crown Point Path*

Along with the four practice procedures mentioned above, you can also extend the exhalation path to reach the crown point, which means that you can inhale through the nostrils and down to the tan t'ien, and then send the turbine-like flow of ch'i along the spinal column, all the way up to the crown point. You can then reverse the path by exhaling down the spinal column to the tan t'ien and up through the nostrils, or guide the flow from the crown point back to the point between the shoulder blades on the spinal column and then separate the flow, sending it down both arms and down to the center of the palms (the *yun chung*) and outside. On the exhale, the ch'i should be directed alternately along one path and then the other.

6. *Exhale Down to the Sole Path*

Using the procedure for exhalation described thus far, you can also extend your practice by extending the exhale fully and driving the ch'i flow all the way down to the soles of the feet, focusing on the center point of the sole (the *yun-chuan* or "erupting spring"). This process will help to develop more completely the free circulation of the ch'i and, more importantly, will aid in the development of *rooting.* Rooting is an advanced technique which, in the martial art aspect of T'ai Chi, can be a vital factor in determining how well a student has disciplined himself during his training.

7. *The Entire Body Path*

After following all the practice procedures described so far carefully and precisely, you can further your breathing training by extending the ch'i flow throughout the entire body.

As well as carefully observing all the T'ai Chi principles during each portion of practice, you should also realize that: (1) the paths described above are merely imaginary routes that are designed to bring up the substantial feeling of ch'i flow; (2) the physical act of breathing should continue in the same fashion as described at the beginning of each practice procedure; and (3) the imaginary route and inhalation/exhalation movement should be in harmony with each other (i.e., you do not imagine that you are exhaling while you are physically inhaling, or vice versa).

By following these three instructions and practicing the six previously listed procedures, you will develop a total breath-control practice system which will increase the awareness of ch'i within the body. This is known as the "cultivation of the ch'i" in T'ai Chi practice.

Inhalation on the physical level serves as a reminder on the mental level to guide the ch'i to the tan t'ien, where it acquires a turbine-like spin, and then up the spinal column to the crown point. Exhalation is a reminder to guide the ch'i down the back and arms to the center of the palms, through the spinal column, and down the legs to the center of the soles of the feet.

Repeat this process for as long as necessary. If there is still difficulty in sensing the entire breath feeling, or if there seems to be an interruption of the feeling of the ch'i flow at any point along the route, try shaking the body gently and shifting the weight slightly and continuously from side to side.

This should help to build a complete feeling of ch'i circulation in conjunction with physical breathing. With success in this process (known as *ch'i-tone* in T'ai Chi), you will be able to easily circulate the ch'i flow ceaselessly. Eventually, using the mind to guide and control the now-substantial feelings, you will be ready for the condensing breathing practice which is used to generate jing, the internal power.

Having traveled upward through the seven steps, you should then practice a *natural cul-*

tivation stage known as *yan-chi* and described by the late Cheng Man-ch'ing as *wu-wong wu-chu,* which means "Do not ignore your ch'i or try to help its growth."

The apparent paradox of Master Cheng's words bothers beginners who are trying hard to develop the feeling of ch'i within themselves. Perhaps an analogy will be helpful: When you plant a tree, you don't overtend it in order to make it grow faster; but you don't completely forget about it either. Proper and constant care is the best way to make the tree grow. Similarly, Master Cheng described the daily growth of ch'i as being as little as a thin layer of paper. "To stack it up as high as a skyscraper," he said, "will take you a good several years."

Concentration Development

In attempting to be "good" at T'ai Chi, one should focus on mental development and internal work. If one has tried all the proper practice steps and has still failed to achieve substantial progress, it is probably due to lack of concentration. It is concentration that serves as the medium to increase the feeling of awareness of ch'i.

One may be sincere and dedicated to the T'ai Chi principles and still not pay attention to what should be done. Eventually, T'ai Chi becomes a routine daily exercise. Once while chatting with me, Cheng Man-ch'ing criticized his students for not paying attention to what they were doing; they were not concentrating on the proper material. In this way students make unnecessary errors, even though they practice with dedication.

Hundreds of T'ai Chi enthusiasts practice their art diligently and sincerely for years, but without satisfactory achievement. Even under the supervision of a qualified master, a student could receive little benefit from T'ai Chi training. This is because, when dealing with invisible energy, it is very easy to mislead oneself or to be fooled by one's own feeling if one does not pay proper attention.

In the beginning it is imperative that a great deal of attention be paid to the mind, the body, and the new forms that have to be learned. As time goes on, however, the forms become much easier. The physical movements require so little effort, in fact, that they can be performed without the student having to pay any attention to what is being done. All too often, T'ai Chi becomes a mechanical routine, and the student ignores the important mental aspects of the discipline completely. This attitude, which develops gradually, can paralyze mental development.

In T'ai Chi practice, concentration on the entire body and mind is needed to achieve a state that increases ch'i awareness and serves as the foundation for progress in the art. *The T'ai Chi Classics* say that "whether you are doing a Ward Off Form, a Rollback Form, Press, or Push, you should concentrate on the real practice." Master Cheng explains:

"You have to look into its real meaning instead of paying no attention to what you are doing; otherwise a Ward Off Form won't be a Ward Off Form, and a Rollback Form won't be a Rollback Form any more." Because the true T'ai Chi practitioner works by exercising the mind and body together, not paying attention to what you are doing means that you won't be in the *state* of T'ai Chi. You will only be performing a T'ai Chi–like exercise, which cannot be considered true T'ai Chi practice.

To increase the ability to concentrate, beginners should use imagination in practice. For instance, students should try to imagine that there is an opponent in front of them as they do the Ward Off, Press, or Push forms. Gradually the student will learn to concentrate mind and body totally without the aid of the imaginary opponent. Thus a total concentration on ch'i movement will be generated, which will in turn increase the awareness of ch'i within the body.

Physical discomfort usually disturbs concentration. The student should therefore determine the cause of the discomfort and try to correct the situation. However, the beginner should expect a certain amount of discomfort to occur during the first stage of training in the T'ai Chi Form. As the training progresses, the discomfort should gradually disappear—usually after several weeks of practice. When the forms can be performed comfortably at will, the student should try to advance to a more meditative stage.

Total involvement in T'ai Chi, both mentally and physically, is the only way to increase concentration and consequently increase the awareness of ch'i within the body. Master Cheng once told me that if a person can't enjoy being drunk, then he is truly drunk, so drinking has no meaning at all. In other words, if a person is able to enjoy the sensation of drunkenness, he is not really drunk at all. This illustrates the two stages of T'ai Chi practice. At first you are conscious of the feelings; later you are no longer aware. This is the stage to reach. You should be in it and of it. This is true T'ai Chi; then you are really practicing correctly.

Coordination Practice

Ch'i flows within the body and acts as the source and meaning of life. As mentioned previously, any interference will cause blockage and so reduce the effectiveness of the function of ch'i. When one's ch'i is operating below its normal level, sickness occurs and one cannot sense the feeling of ch'i flow at all. Even under normal conditions, one can cause the ch'i flow to become gradually reduced, simply by not achieving proper mental and physical coordination.

According to T'ai Chi tradition, the newborn baby is an example of total relaxation and coordination. Each action is carried out as one mentally and physically integrated unity, in one complete motion. For example, when crying, the infant uses its whole body to cry; when eating or moving, all parts of the body coordinate for a totality of action. As time passes and the child learns the sophisticated ways of civilization, he or she loses the natural ability to coordinate. Gradually, the inherent integrated feeling is lost, and the flow of ch'i is reduced proportionately.

In T'ai Chi, coordination is considered to be one of the key factors in the achievement of ch'i awareness. The coordination of internal power (*jen-jing*) has been misunderstood and misinterpreted throughout the entire history of T'ai Chi. If a person does not understand the real meaning of relaxation (*shoong*), then that person can also not understand the meaning of coordination.

In lay terms, coordination means involving the total mind and total body, which function in the proper order. When picking up a pen from a desk, a person will unconsciously stretch out an arm and grasp the pen with the hand. This action requires no concentration, so none is used. It is quite a different matter, however, if the same person were to move a desk through a narrow doorway. In that instance, the person would be required to use a great deal of coordination of mind and body. Not only would every part of the body be brought to bear in order to handle the weight and mass of the desk, but total concentration would also be needed to solve the problem of getting the desk to fit through the doorway.

When practicing T'ai Chi, and especially when performing the meditative movements, a total involvement of mind and body, functioning in the proper order, results in a totally coordinated condition. This means that one does not make mere local movements of the body, such as only moving the hand or the leg; nor does one make meaningless movements, such as moving the body in the correct form but without giving thought to each movement.

For example, when performing the Ward Off Form, the hands, arms, torso, and so on should move in a coordinated manner—a manner that best suits the meaning of the form. If some portion of the body fails to perform in a manner that assists the movement, or if the body performs the pattern of the form without the mind being engaged, the result will be confusion and disorder. Poor coordination will interfere with the free flow of internal energy and gradually reduce the awareness of ch'i circulation. Thus the development of ch'i will be weakened.

In *The T'ai Chi Classics,* Chang San-feng says, "From foot to leg and waist, the entire body should move as one unit and coordinate with one ch'i." The entire body should be in coordination with the totality of the ch'i. The body should be able to connect and integrate into one complete system, instead of operating as "scattered pieces." A beginner in T'ai Chi, then, should look closely at the true meaning of coordination.

Besides being an element of the practice routine, coordination should be practiced in daily life. For example, each time you go to answer the telephone, the entire body moves forward to pick up the receiver. As the receiver is lifted from the cradle, you should imagine that it is very heavy and fragile and so requires your full attention and the entire strength of your body to lift it. The same type of practice can be applied when you use your silverware at meals, and so on. Moving the body as one complete unit aids in the free, unobstructed flow of ch'i. Therefore, constantly practicing in this way will serve as a reminder to your mind and body systems and will increase natural coordination and, consequently, the awareness of ch'i within the body.

Meditation and Imagination

Initiation of the feeling of ch'i flow depends a great deal on the use of meditation and, to a certain extent, on the use of imagination. If the four practices described in this chapter thus far have been followed and the results are still not satisfactory, the following steps will help to increase the awareness of ch'i.

Step One

In a relaxed sitting posture, raise both hands above the head and extend them out to the side, so that the arms form a V shape. The wrists are relaxed and have a slight natural curve; the hands are relaxed, with the fingers slightly bent in a natural position. Nothing is stretched to its fullest extent or held rigid. The eyes are closed. The tongue is rolled up behind the ridge on the roof of the mouth. The toes are pointed slightly inward.

Concentrate for about a minute on feeling something flowing down from the fingertips to the shoulders. Then gently drop your arms. Repeat this practice several times and continue using it as part of the practice routine until awareness of the flowing feeling develops.

Step Two

After practicing the above step several times, you can decrease the amount of imagination needed to produce the slow, floating feeling. Gradually you will develop the ability to use the mind to control the speed of the flow, making it go fast, slow, or even forcing it to stop at a given spot and then continue on its downward path. Be extremely careful with this step. Bear in mind at all times the T'ai

Chi principles. Keep the body relaxed. Tensing up the arms in an attempt to strengthen the muscles and thus alter the flow feelings will lead to great difficulties later on.

Step Three

After achieving success in the process described in the first two steps, extend the practice as follows. Relax the arms and gently place them in front of the stomach with the palms facing upward and the fingertips touching each other. The elbows are slightly bent. Applying the same flowing feeling, and again using your mind to guide the flow, circulate the energy from the fingertips along both arms, upward to the shoulders. Finally, have the energy meet at the center point between the shoulder blades. Repeat this practice many times, until the feeling becomes substantial.

Step Four

You may also expand the practice described above in the following way. Move the feeling from the point between the shoulder blades down the spinal column, through the legs to the feet. Or, send the flow to the crown point, through the face, or to the tan t'ien area. This step may take several months of faithful, persistent practice.

Step Five

After developing the feeling of circulating the energy to all parts of the body, concentrate on the entire body. The circulation of the energy feeling will then assist the ch'i to flow with it, and it will grow strong within and throughout the body.

T'ai Chi Meditative Form Practice

Another way to increase the awareness of one's ch'i is through the practice of T'ai Chi forms in a meditative manner. As mentioned previously, if one merely performs the T'ai Chi movements physically, it will just be a T'ai Chi–like exercise, and not T'ai Chi at all. To move your body in T'ai Chi forms, you must meditate and drive the energy feeling with your mind, even if it is only from imagination. When practice is repeated over a long period of time, it will help the ch'i to flow in a T'ai Chi way, which means that the entire body will move as one unit. As soon as the ch'i flows, you will easily become aware of its existence.

T'ai Chi masters traditionally taught their students to use meditative practice to develop ch'i awareness. Such a training program would require a longer period of time to complete than other methods; in this way the master would have time to observe the student's attitude and personality and determine whether or not to continue the program of instruction. Otherwise, the student could develop ch'i awareness for unacceptable reasons, such as poor attitude, ego, or wanting to be stronger than others. If such motivations emerged, the teacher would discontinue instruction without giving the student such key techniques as condensing breathing, which is the main process used to convert ch'i into internal power.

This instruction method was especially used in the late 1930s. Master Shen Tongsheng, the last living prominent T'ai Chi master from the previous generation, once told me that his teachers gave him many tests to prove his sincerity and personality. According to Master Shen, the simplest, most basic way to bring up one's awareness of ch'i is as follows: "Even if you do not practice one hundred percent correctly, you continue to practice the Meditative Form for at least ten years. You should then be able to feel the ch'i; it's only a matter of time." He added, "But even though you may develop ch'i awareness and control through a different method, you still require daily practice of the T'ai Chi Meditative Movement to increase the ch'i volume, which is beneficial to your condensing practice."

Two-Person Practice

If a student has failed to achieve success in the development of ch'i awareness by other means, even through the practice of the T'ai Chi Meditative Movement, the master will introduce two-person practice. In fact, any student, beginning or advanced, who intends to succeed in martial arts through T'ai Chi practice needs two-person practice in order to increase the awareness of ch'i and to learn the different types of feelings and control required. Push Hands, Rolling Hands, Ta-Lu, and so on will help the student to sense the different pressures and speeds, to gain control, and to realize how to maneuver the body in a flowing, coordinated manner, thus increasing the awareness of ch'i.

Advanced students should practice a great deal of Rolling Hands to increase the flow of ch'i and also to communicate with another's ch'i feelings. With intensive practice under a master's guidance, one can develop very strong awareness of the ch'i not only in oneself, but also in another person. A high degree of sensitivity will be developed which can, through physical contact, determine the magnitude, wavelength, and direction of another person's ch'i.

All the different types of internal power (jing) are developed through control of ch'i by the process known as condensing breathing. Jing can be classified according to the way ch'i is controlled. *Sticking Power,* for instance, is a magnetic type of power which is derived from the reversal of the ch'i flow.

Auxiliary Training

Throughout the history of T'ai Chi, certain instruments, such as the sword, knife, and staff, have been widely used to help improve T'ai Chi development. Of these auxiliary practices, T'ai Chi Sword is considered the most efficient means of increasing one's awareness of ch'i. The sword, with its balanced weight and characteristic flexibility, is designed to serve as an extension of the body. The practice of T'ai Chi Sword requires a great deal of concentration and body coordination and so produces a high degree of ch'i awareness.

With the lifestyle imposed by today's industrial society, the practice of T'ai Chi Sword may seem impractical. However, there are great benefits to be reaped from this practice, and it should be considered as one of the very important aspects of the study of T'ai Chi. For further information about T'ai Chi Sword practice, the student is advised to consult with a qualified instructor.

One important note about auxiliary training is that the training equipment should be well made and custom-adjusted to a perfect balance and flexibility. A wooden sword or one made of cast metal is not recommended as a substitute for the real equipment.

3

T'AI CHI CLASSICS I

Treatise by
Master Chang San-feng

(CA. 1200 C.E.)

氣宜鼓盪

神宜內歛

"The internal energy should be extended,
vibrated like the beat of a drum. The spirit should be
condensed in toward the center of your body."

Once you begin to move, the entire body must be light and limber. Each part of your body should be connected to every other part.

In T'ai Chi practice, the entire body should coordinate into one complete unit. Once you begin to move, the entire body should move, and not just the hand, leg, elbow, and so on. As a beginner you should observe this principle at all times.

The universe moves and exercises its influence in a coordinated manner. For example, when the earth rotates the entire planet moves. Imagine what would happen if only part of the earth rotated while the rest of the planet remained stationary. As the system of balance and harmony was upset, drastic changes would occur throughout the universe.

T'ai Chi was created as a system of mental and physical discipline which human beings could understand and follow, and which is based on universal principles of balance and harmony. When you practice T'ai Chi, the first basic principle that you follow is: "Once you begin to move, the entire body must move as one."

Merely moving an arm or a leg is not practicing in a T'ai Chi manner. The body must be coordinated, relaxed, comfortable, peaceful, and mentally alert. In this way you will be able to maneuver the body in any direction, at will; when the mind wishes to move, the body will instantaneously follow its command.

A mistake often made by students who are new to the art of T'ai Chi is that of allowing the various parts of the body to move separately, in an uncoordinated manner. This is due to the fact that the parts of the body are not connected. When the hand moves, the rest of the body should respond in a totally coordinated manner. This will result in a well-controlled movement and help in the development of internal energy, which will eventually lead to the process of internal power projection.

The internal energy should be extended, vibrated like the beat of a drum. The spirit should be condensed in toward the center of your body.

Let us review here the important factors involved in the exercise of ch'i when practicing the T'ai Chi Form, as discussed in chapter 2. You should drive your internal energy outward from the center of the tan t'ien and extend it with sufficient pressure (not too much and not too little) so that the tension upon its surface is like that on the head of a drum. The ch'i will then vibrate like the beat of a drum when set in motion. The most important principle in the cultivation of ch'i is that you should extend your ch'i to the maximum margin of allowable pressure.

Cultivating your ch'i will also stimulate the power of your spirit, which should be drawn inward toward your center point and condensed into the bone marrow. Stronger ch'i will help to elevate the power and the amount of the spirit. Do not let the spirit extend outward and get lost. Rather, let it be condensed inward and recycled.

When performing T'ai Chi, it should be perfect; allow no defect. The form should be smooth with no unevenness, and continuous, allowing no interruptions.

When you consider T'ai Chi as a discipline art and yourself as a martial artist, your attitude should be that of looking for perfection—which means that you continue to improve your study and practice until there is no defect.

The T'ai Chi meditative movements must be very smooth and even, just as if you were trying to draw a perfect circle without the aid of an instrument. You begin with a rough draft and try to draw as evenly and smoothly as possible in every direction. Although a perfect circle may only be possible in theory, as you continue working toward this goal you will be acting in a manner that is close to the required smoothness and evenness.

The internal energy, ch'i, roots at the feet, then transfers through the legs and is controlled from the waist, moving eventually through the back to the arms and fingertips.

Master Yang Chien-hou (1839–1917), son of Master Yang Lu-chan, liked to remind his disciples of this principle many times during

 his daily T'ai Chi instruction.

After achieving some success in ch'i awareness practice, the T'ai Chi student should learn how to lower his ch'i feeling down to the

ground and then project it upward from his feet through his legs. Therefore, in T'ai Chi practice, always keep your knees bent slightly to allow flexibility; never straighten your legs completely. This will allow the vibration of your internal energy to be transmitted from your feet through your knees to your waist.

Note that *The T'ai Chi Classics* use the term *root,* which emphasizes the importance of the feet. Both feet must always stay firmly attached to the ground, as strongly as the roots of a big tree. Also, the feeling of internal energy must penetrate deep into the ground, instead of merely being attached to the surface.

After projecting the ch'i upward, your waist serves as a transmitter; it controls, guides, and distributes the direction and amount of internal energy.

Keep your back and your entire torso in a vertical position, to allow the vibrations to travel freely upward through your back to your shoulders. Keep your shoulders completely relaxed to allow the transmission of ch'i down to your elbows and up to your fingertips. Always keep your elbows dropped and relaxed; your wrists are relaxed, but not limp.

> When transferring the ch'i from your feet to your waist, your body must operate as if all the parts were one; this allows you to move forward and backward freely with control of balance and position. Failure to do this causes loss of control of the entire body system. The only cure for such a problem is an examination of the stance.

Ch'i carries tremendous amounts of vibration, requiring a high degree of coordination of the entire body. Your torso and limbs, your hands and legs, must be coordinated both physically and mentally with every other part of the body. All the parts should relate to each other as one inseparable unit, especially when you transfer your ch'i from the root upward. Success in this will allow you to maneuver your entire body—forward, backward, upward, downward—at will. You will be able to control any situation.

If the body is not coordinated, you will not be able to control your body system. According to the advice given in this T'ai Chi treatise (added at a later date by an unknown T'ai Chi master), "The only cure for such a problem is an examination of the stance."

Just as a weak foundation is unable to support a tall, strong building, a poor stance in T'ai Chi form will lead to poor coordination of the entire body, and this will prevent the student from being able to maneuver his body as one integrated unit.

Application of these principles promotes the flowing T'ai Chi movement in any direction: forward, backward, right side, and left side.

When you perform your T'ai Chi movements in a totally coordinated manner, your body is light and limber, and each part of your body connects to every other part. Your

T'ai Chi form is very smooth and continuous, your ch'i vibrations are extended, and your spirit is condensed and centered.

The ch'i transfers from your feet upward through your legs to your waist, and eventually through your back to your arms and fingertips. This allows you to develop your mind to guide your body, so that you can move in any direction at will: forward, backward, to the right or left, up or down.

In all of this, you must emphasize the use of the mind in controlling your movements, rather than the mere use of the external muscles. You should also follow the T'ai Chi principle of opposites: when you move upward, the mind must be aware of down; when moving forward, the mind also thinks of moving back; when shifting to the left side, the mind should simultaneously notice the right side—so that if the mind is going up, it is also going down.

T'ai Chi emphasizes the development of the mind rather than the muscles, since the mind can be developed infinitely, beyond any limits of time and space.

In T'ai Chi practice you allow your mind to follow the T'ai Chi principle of opposites: the principle of Yin and Yang. Physically, your body can move in only one direction at a time—for example, a move to the right side. Yet in such a move there are other possibilities: moving to the left side, upward, downward, backward, forward. Thus, when you move in one direction, your mind should be simultaneously aware of the other possibilities.

When you have achieved the practice of yielding and totally relaxing yourself, your body will be able to respond freely to the direction of the mind. Theoretically, this type of training will allow the physical body to move as rapidly as the body's mental processes. Although in actuality limitations on physical movement may exist, the discipline will result in a body that is more limber and movements that are more controlled.

> Such principles relate to T'ai Chi movement in the same way that uprooting an object, and thereby destroying its foundation, will make the object fall sooner.

In the practice of T'ai Chi movement, Uprooting Power follows the principle presented previously: the most efficient method of destroying an object's foundation is to uproot it. T'ai Chi masters have widely emphasized this principle in relation to Push Hands practice. By allowing the mind to focus downward, the opponent will resist in an upward direction and therefore allow you to uproot him easily and efficiently.

> Besides clearly separating the positive and negative from one another, you should also clearly locate the substan-

tial and insubstantial. When the entire body is integrated with all parts connected together, it becomes a vast connection of positive and negative energy units. Each positive and negative unit of energy should be connected to every other unit and permit no interruption among them.

Since the Yin/Yang theory is the main principle of T'ai Chi philosophy, when you perform T'ai Chi movements the entire body must separate clearly into the positive and negative portions. For example, when your weight is placed more heavily on your right foot, the right side of your body will be substantial (positive, or Yang) and the left side insubstantial (negative, or Yin). When you are moving forward, the front side of your body will be Yang and the rear or back portion of your body will be Yin. Conversely, when you are moving backward, your back will be Yang and your front will be Yin.

If your hand is moving forward, with the palm facing you, the back of your hand will be Yang and the palm will be Yin. In relation to your arm, the entire hand would be considered Yang and the arm, as it followed the forward direction of your hand, would be Yin. In relation to your other hand and arm, the entire moving hand and arm would be Yang while the other hand and arm would be Yin.

The same principle can be applied to the entire body. The body consists of a large number of positive and negative energy units. Each small unit of Yin and Yang must connect to every other unit in a coordinated manner, with no interruption among them, in order to maneuver the entire body in a balanced Yin/Yang manner. Connecting to each other also means coordinating with each other: neither the Yin nor the Yang can act independently, without regard for the other's motion.

In Long Forms your body should move like the rhythmic flow of water on a river or like the rolling waves of the ocean.

When you study T'ai Chi, each meditative movement is a complete unit within the T'ai Chi system. As you combine your forms into a larger and longer system, you should regard all of the forms as having become one long form, just as, if you were to pour many cups of water into a large container, you would then have one container of water, instead of many separate, smaller units.

When you perform the forms you should also allow your internal energy to drive your entire body to flow, so that it moves continuously, like water flowing in a river or like the rolling waves of the ocean.

In the Long Form, Ward Off, Rollback, Press, Push, Roll-Pull, Split, Elbow, and Lean Forward are called *the forms of the Eight Diagram (Pakua)*, the move-

ment encompassing the eight directions. In stance, moving forward,
backward, to the right side, to the left
side, and staying in the center are
called *the Five-Style Steps.* Ward Off,
Rollback, Press, and Push are called
the four cardinal directions. Roll-Pull,
Split, Elbow, and Lean Forward forms
are called *the four diagonals.* Forward,
backward, to the left side, to the right
side, and center are called *metal, wood,
water, fire,* and *earth,* respectively.
When combined, these forms are
called *the thirteen original styles of
T'ai Chi.*

The T'ai Chi Form originated as the thirteen
postures of meditation. These are the eight
postures, or directions—the Ward Off, Rollback, Press, and Push forms comprising the
four cardinal directions, and the Roll-Pull,
Split, Elbow, and Lean Forward forms, comprising the four diagonal directions—in

combination with the five different ways to maneuver the eight meditative postures: forward, backward, to the left side, to the right side, and staying still in the center.

Through observation, the ancient Chinese defined the nature of human life according to five categories: metal, wood, water, fire, and earth. Metal represents hardness and penetration; as you move forward you act with the character of metal. Wood represents flexibility combined with strength; it is yielding and growing. When you move backward, your action has the character of wood. Fire and water act in opposite directions, but both are characterized by aggressiveness and pliability. They are yielding, piercing, uncertain, and powerful. When you move to the right or left side, you embody these attributes. Earth represents stability, immobility, motherhood, the center, the calmness of the origin. When you remain in the center, you adopt the nature of earth.

太極拳經

王宗岳

*"T'ai Chi Classics of
Master Wong Chung-yua"*

4

T'AI CHI CLASSICS II

Treatise by
Master Wong Chung-yua

(CA. 1600 C.E.)

T'ai Chi is born out of infinity. It is the origin of the positive and the negative. When T'ai Chi is in motion, the positive and the negative separate; when T'ai Chi stops, the positive and negative integrate.

It is believed that this classical T'ai Chi treatise was written by Master Wong Chung-yua, who was the master of Ch'en Chang-hsing, the originator of the Yang system.

Approximately four hundred years ago, Master Wong described T'ai Chi using the Yin/Yang theory. He believed that the Yin/Yang principle originated from *not-being,* and that everything in our universe follows this principle.

Neither Yin, the negative, nor Yang, the positive, can exist independently. When these equal-but-opposite energies separate, the T'ai Chi is in motion. When they unite, the T'ai Chi is in stillness.

According to modern knowledge, everything is fundamentally constructed from atoms. To manifest in material existence these atoms must combine negative and positive powers in order to balance opposing energies. This forms a stability so that matter can exist.

Such principles were discovered and emphasized at the dawn of Chinese civilization, as T'ai Chi philosophy. Books such as the *I Ching (Book of Changes)* sought to describe and explain the nature of the universe, including human life, as the interchange of the essence of balanced but opposite powers. When studying T'ai Chi, it is important to understand the dynamic relationship of the Yin and Yang energies.

When practicing T'ai Chi, doing too much is the same as doing too little. When the body is in motion, it should follow the curve to extend the movements.

The Yin/Yang theory also emphasizes the principle of harmony and balance. Too much

Yin or too much Yang will destroy the harmonious balance of energies. Whether performing the meditative movements or practicing two-person Push Hands, doing too much is as bad as doing too little.

In the practice of T'ai Chi, it is important to follow the principle of moderation. In some forms it is required that your posture be lowered or your arms be stretched to some degree. Practicing these forms correctly is a way of developing harmony in your entire body system: if you stretch your arm too much or not enough, or lower your body too far or not far enough, you will lose the meaning of being in harmony, whether with yourself or your opponent. Similarly, any unnecessary movement, or failure to move at a critical time, is considered too much or too little.

Since the most harmonious and natural line between two points is a graceful and evenly rounded curve, your entire body should follow such curves. This is a guideline for how to extend your movements. Your body movements should be not too fast, not too slow, not too rigid, not too limp. This is the T'ai Chi principle of *not too much and not too little*.

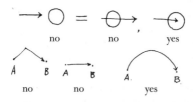

If your opposite side is hard, change your own side to make it soft. This is called *following*. If your opponent is moving and you adhere to him while following in the same direction, it is called *sticking*. Then you are *attached* to your opponent: when he moves faster, you also move faster; when he moves slower, you move slower, thereby matching his movement.

Master Wong emphasized the principles of *following, sticking,* and *attaching.* In two-person practice, these different but related internal powers are developed through sensitivity discipline.

Following Power. In two-person practice, when you sense that your opponent is putting pressure on you, adjust and change your own side to make it soft, and yield to him. Your response is in the T'ai Chi manner: not too much, not too little. When your pressure has adequately adjusted to your opponent's level, this kind of sensitivity and controlling ability is called Following Power.

Sticking Power. When you constantly increase your sensitivity and ability to follow your opponent and are able to adhere to his pressure in whatever direction he moves, you will then develop the mental ability of controlling your body and its movement to act in accord with your opponent. This ability, known as Sticking Power, acts and feels like magnetic power. Sticking Power is required for Free Hand practice in martial arts, in order to be able to contact and control the opponent during the initial actions.

Attaching Power. After having developed Following Power and Sticking Power, you can learn to further respond to and match your opponent's moves, whether fast or slow. This ability is known as Attaching Power.

Regardless of your opponent's actions, the principle of your response remains the same. Once this type of movement has become your own, you will understand internal power.

In addition to developing and cultivating awareness of the internal energy, ch'i, it will be helpful to understand internal power, jing.

Initially, you should develop Sticking Power; then develop Following as well as Attaching Power. After achieving this, regardless of your opponent's actions, you will follow him and match him in perfect harmony; you may control your opponent at will. The principle of your response to your opponent remains that of Yin/Yang balance and harmony.

After coming to an understanding of the internal power of movement, you can approach the theory of natural awareness. Natural awareness is developed through practice over a long period of time; you cannot reach a sudden understanding of natural awareness without proper practice for an extended length of time.

The T'ai Chi system is based on the natural law of harmony and balance. Through the development of internal power you can obtain a full understanding of its character and properties, which will serve as a bridge to the stage of *natural awareness*.

According to Master Wong, the important point is that the natural awareness stage requires a long period of practice in T'ai Chi. After proper practice for an extended length of time, even though you may not be able to feel the gradual progression in your conscious mind, the accumulation of internal power will suddenly turn into a higher level of achievement, known as natural awareness. As an analogy, when heating water to its boiling point, it does not boil up gradually, but slowly accumulates heat and then suddenly begins to boil after reaching the proper temperature.

Proper practice means practicing under the supervision of a qualified master; practicing for an extended length of time means continuously practicing without interruption. As in the analogy of heating water to a boiling point, one's development requires constant, uninterrupted "heat."

When you practice T'ai Chi, you should relax the neck and suspend the head, as if from a height above you.

Internal power should sink to the lower part of the abdomen. Your posture should keep to the center. Do not lean in any direction. Your movements should be constantly changing from the substantial to the insubstantial. If your left side feels heavy, you should make your left side light. If your right side feels heavy, you should make your right side disappear.

T'ai Chi practice involves the development of ch'i, which serves as the energy to propel the internal power. Therefore, in any process of projecting your power, it is very important to keep your head suspended upward and your neck relaxed. Your neck will then serve as a cushion, filtering the vibrations to your head. In addition, this technique will allow the spiritual power to develop more rapidly.

Ch'i originates from the lower abdominal area (ten t'ien). Without proper discipline and cultivation it declines before you reach adulthood. Either through the use of imagination or through the aid of inhalation exercises, bring feeling down to the lower part of your abdomen. This will help increase the development and awareness of your ch'i.

The T'ai Chi meditative movements will allow your ch'i to flow and vibrate freely. You should keep your posture in the center, and in vertical alignment. Leaning in any direction will cause blockage of your ch'i.

According to the Yin/Yang theory, Yin constantly changes to Yang, and Yang constantly changes to Yin. Your T'ai Chi meditative movements should follow the same principle: substantial changes to insubstantial, and vice versa. When one part feels heavy, make it feel light or make it disappear.

Make your opponent feel that when he looks upward, you are much taller, and when he looks downward, you are much lower. When he moves forward,

he should feel that he cannot reach you, and when he retreats, he should feel that he has nowhere to escape to.

In two-person practice (Rolling Hands, Free Hands, Moving Steps, etc.), besides applying Sticking Power, Following Power, and Attaching Power, you should also observe the Yin/Yang theory. Mentally follow your opponent's moves and react in the opposite direction or in the opposite manner from what he expects.

When he looks upward, you are responding as if you are much taller than he expects; when he looks downward, you are acting as if you are much lower than he anticipates. Similarly, when he approaches, make him feel that he cannot reach you, that you are farther away than he expects. When he retreats, make him feel that he has nowhere to escape to, because you are faster and longer than he anticipates. To achieve this ability one should practice a great deal of Hands Attaching, Moving For-

ward and Backward Steps, Attaching Steps,
and the Five-Style Steps.

> **Your body's sensitivity should be such
> that you are aware of the tiniest
> feather brushing against your skin.
> Even the mosquito finds no place to
> land on you without causing you to
> move. Then there will be no way for
> your opponent to detect or control
> you, but you will be aware of your op-
> ponent and control him.**

When practicing the T'ai Chi Meditative
Movement, try to develop an ultimate sensitivity toward and awareness of your mind and the
natural conditions surrounding you. To achieve
this you should understand the theory of Yin/
Yang harmony and balance, as well as the philosophy of yielding and neutralizing.

Constant practice in this direction will
cause you to achieve a high level of sensitivity
to external stimuli. This achievement is described in *The T'ai Chi Classics* as the ability

to detect even the tiniest feather or the smallest mosquito touching your skin. In addition to developing Sticking Power, Following Power, and Attaching Power, you will then be able to understand and fully control your opponent. And there will be no way for your opponent to detect and control you.

For a beginner, the best way to develop this ability is through either meditation practice or Push Hands practice with a higher-level student or an instructor.

If you achieve this level of sensitivity, there is no force that will defeat you. There are thousands of methods and techniques in the martial arts. Regardless of the techniques and postures employed, most depend on physical condition (strong destroys weak) and speed (fast defeats slow), so that the weak must fall to the strong and the slow must lose to the fast. This, however, is dependent on physical ability

and does not relate to the discipline that we now discuss.

Accomplishment in the level of sensitivity just discussed will help you to develop the internal power that will guide your body to respond properly to your opponent. This energy will yield to force and control the attack. There will be no way for the opponent to defeat you. However, since this accomplishment requires long periods of practice and the theory behind it is a paradox to our commonsense logic, this type of training has tended to be ignored, and a more physical type of conditioning has been emphasized. But training that depends solely on physical ability has nothing to do with the discipline and development of the mind.

Look into the technique of using four ounces of energy to control the force of a thousand pounds. Such techniques as these do not depend on brute force to overcome.

"Four ounces of strength to defeat one thousand pounds" is a traditional way of describing efficiency and superiority in martial art systems. Obviously, such an efficient use of energy requires highly sophisticated techniques, so that the four ounces are repeatedly increased and accumulated.

Observe the ability of the old man who can successfully defend himself against many opponents at once. This proves that speed does not determine victory.

Besides the ability to properly utilize internal power, proper timing also serves as an important factor in overcoming the opponent. This is illustrated here with the example of an old man who is able to defend himself successfully against many opponents at one time, proving that speed does not determine victory.

Proper movements at a slow speed make more sense than faster movements improperly executed. In T'ai Chi terminology, *speed* refers to pacing, to moving slow or fast or not at all. It involves anticipation and awareness. So-called faster speed is only measured relative to the change of pace.

When you practice T'ai Chi, you should stand with your posture balanced like a scale. When you move, your movements should revolve as effortlessly as the turning of a wheel.

In T'ai Chi practice, the entire body must be coordinated as one complete unit. Your body will then be able to follow your mind, moving in any direction you wish. In addition, to ensure that your movement is totally harmonious and balanced, you must keep your standing posture as balanced as a scale. This will allow you to instantly detect any change of balance, either in yourself or in your opponent.

Your movement should also follow a graceful curved line, to allow your ch'i to flow freely. Let your movement revolve as smoothly as the turning of a wheel. In other words, your movement should circulate ceaselessly and evenly, without interruption or imbalance.

> Following the changing situation, you move as is necessary. If you are unable to respond in this way you will become double-weighted. Often martial artists who have practiced for years still cannot move properly and so cannot follow the flow of their opponent's movement. This is essentially because they are hindered by their mistake of double-weightedness.

When practicing T'ai Chi, doing too much is as bad as doing too little. This principle also applies to making an adequate response to your opponent. When the situation changes, you should follow the change adequately. You only move when it is necessary;

then you can be in harmony with the changing situation and in control of it.

For example, when your opponent moves rapidly, the situation may call for you to respond slowly. It is unnecessary for you to respond quickly, even though your opponent's initial action was at a fast speed. Or, when a changing situation does not require any movement from you, it is necessary for you to remain still.

Failure to respond to the opponent properly will result in awkward mobility, known as *double-weightedness*. This means you are constantly distributing your weight evenly on both feet, due to your hesitation to respond properly.

If you practice T'ai Chi for years and still encounter difficulty in allowing your movements to flow freely with those of your opponent, you should observe the above principle. Single-handed Push Hands practice and the forward and backward movements of the

Five-Style Steps practice with a senior student will help you to correct these problems.

> To avoid double-weightedness you should further understand that positive and negative must complement each other. Then you will understand the flow of internal power, and, having repeatedly practiced and refined your technique and explored your own awareness, you can use and control your internal power at will.
>
> The T'ai Chi principle is as simple as this: yield yourself and follow the external forces. Instead of doing this, most people ignore such obvious and simple principles and search for a more remote and impractical method. This is the so-called inches mistake, which, when allowed to develop, becomes the distance of thousands of miles.
>
> All disciples of T'ai Chi should be aware of this and study diligently.

Master Wong regards the principle of T'ai Chi to be a simple one: yield yourself to the forces of the universe. This may appear to be a paradox, because we are born to grow and expand. Certain degrees of ego and aggressiveness propel and motivate our lives. It definitely is difficult to comprehend the idea of yielding ourselves to the universe.

A simple analogy will help to illustrate this basic principle. If a sealed bottle of water is thrown into a lake, the water in the bottle does not change. But if you pour the water from the bottle directly into the lake, it becomes the water of the lake, instead of the water of the bottle.

In your life, if you yield yourself and follow the universal natural power, you soon will be part of the entire universe. The same principle applies to T'ai Chi martial art practice: after you yield to your opponent you will soon become more powerful than him, because your opponent's force will be under your control, and you will be able to utilize his force as if it belonged to you.

A beginner of T'ai Chi should practice the meditative movements and, under the supervision of a qualified instructor, study a great deal of two-person practice methods and techniques, constantly correcting and adjusting even minor mistakes. Otherwise, after a long period of development, the practice will lead to total error.

5

T'AI CHI
CLASSICS III

Treatise by
Master Wu Yu-hsiang

(1812–1880 C.E.)

十三勢
行功心解

"Heartfelt explanation of the
internal exercise of the
thirteen postures"

Use your mind to exercise your internal energy. Let the internal energy sink and be attached to your body. Eventually, the internal energy can be condensed into the bone marrow.

In the beginning, the ability to concentrate on form practice is very important. The development of concentration will help you to control your mind. Then you can use your mind to increase the awareness of your internal energy, ch'i.

After long periods of practice of internal energy awareness, you will be able to command your mind to guide your internal energy to any part of your body at will. Moreover, you will be able to direct the internal energy to sink and be attached to your entire body. The ability to use your mind to exercise your internal energy is the gate into the internal work known as *nei-kong*.

In advanced stages one can condense the internal energy into the bone marrow throughout the body and generate the ch'i into the high-frequency vibrations known as the internal power, jing.

Drive the internal energy to move your entire body; make certain that the internal energy circulates smoothly and completely. Eventually, the internal energy can follow the direction of your will.

The art of T'ai Chi originated from a philosophy based on the Yin/Yang theory. Since this philosophy emphasizes the balance and harmony of the natural universe, and since human beings are part of this universe, the discipline of being mentally and physically in harmony was originally at the center of the art.

Around 1200 C.E., the T'ai Chi theory was described in *The T'ai Chi Classics I* as a way of discipline and meditation for human life. At that time, success in developing internal energy through Taoist meditation formed the basis for the T'ai Chi Meditative Movement.

Over hundreds of years of development and through many varying approaches to the study process, students came to reverse the proper procedure. In search of an "easier" approach, students began to copy the movements without practicing meditation or internal energy development.

Therefore, around 1850 C.E., Master Wu Yu-hsiang wrote a treatise advising students that to practice T'ai Chi properly, one must drive the internal energy to move the entire body, instead of just copying the T'ai Chi Movement and trying to develop the internal energy afterward. He also advised that one should make certain that the internal energy circulates through the body smoothly and completely, so that it will guide the body to perform the T'ai Chi Meditative Movement gracefully and effortlessly. After developing internal energy, the practitioner can guide the movement in any direction at will.

If essence and spirit can be raised, then there is no need for concern with being slow and awkward; this is called extending and suspending the crown point.

In addition to internal energy development, an important factor affecting the practice and progress of one's T'ai Chi study is the discipline of the essence and spirit. According to Master Wu, your essence and spirit must be raised so that your T'ai Chi movements will be able to flow freely, without being slow and awkward. This refers to using imaging power to direct these two energies, an awareness of which should develop through practice. In other words, extend and suspend the crown point, and relax the neck. These physical movements of the external body will assist in raising the essence and spirit.

Extending and suspending the crown point is the proper way to train and to raise your essence and spirit. In T'ai Chi practice, you must always bear this in mind.

> If mind and internal energy can be freely exchanged, then there is much satisfaction in performing smoothly and dynamically; this is called exchanging negative and positive.

After having advised the student to use the mind to direct the internal energy, Master Wu now advises that one's internal energy must be able to convert to a higher form of power and be complementary to the mind. This means that T'ai Chi meditative movements follow the flow of one's internal energy, and the flow of internal energy is commanded by one's mind. As a result, the meditative movements support and modify the mind in a type of feedback process. In other words, when you can exchange the mind and internal energy freely, your T'ai Chi movements will be much smoother and more dynamic.

According to the Yin/Yang theory, Yin (negative) and Yang (positive) attract each other. If we consider the input factor of mind as positive, then the output factor of internal energy will be negative. With the internal energy acting as input—a positive (Yang) factor—the resulting meditative movement will be negative (Yin). Lastly, considering the meditative movement as acting as input (Yang), this then modifies the condition of your mind (Yin). This is called the exchange of negative and positive, the Yin/Yang theory.

When transferring internal power, it should be sunk, attached, relaxed, and completed. The power should also be concentrated in one direction.

The process of converting your internal energy into internal power through the meditation technique known as *condensing breathing* will generate high-frequency, electrical-type pulsing vibrations. You should then organize and control your mind and body to enter the condition of being *sunk*—firmly based and rooted to the ground.

Let the internal power vibrate, attach to your entire body, and connect to your opponent. The structure of your body must be completely relaxed and coordinated. The transfer of power must be completely projected, concentrated in one direction only, in order to allow the vibration of your power to accelerate and exceed the speed of light.

The mind serves as a medium to penetrate the limit of time. Your mind guides the direction of your power. When the mind concentrates in one direction, the acceleration of the vibration, propelled by the mind over the shortest distance, will result in increased effectiveness.

When performing, you should be centered, balanced, stable, and comfortable. You should also control the eight directions.

When performing the T'ai Chi Meditative Movement, regard yourself as always standing at the center of the universe. Each portion and posture of the body must be balanced and coordinated. The flow of your internal energy drives the entire body to move freely; however, it must be under control so that it will be stable and comfortable.

You should also bear in mind that there are eight directions which need to be controlled as you perform the movements. As mentioned in the discussion of Master Chang San-feng's treatise (chapter 3), you should follow the T'ai Chi principle of opposites. At the same time that you focus the mind in one specific direction, you must also be aware of and consider all directions.

Circulating your internal energy is just like guiding a thread through the nine-channeled pearl. Then nothing can block the circulation.

After success in internal energy awareness practice you will learn to circulate internal energy throughout your body. Besides relaxing your entire body as you try to guide your internal energy, you should also bear in mind that you need patience, delicate effort, and concentration, as if guiding a tiny thread through a "nine-channeled pearl," the tiny wooden ball used by young Chinese girls to test and improve their manual dexterity. The "pearl" contains nine small openings leading to criss-crossing channels in the interior of the ball. Any rushed movement or excess pressure in pushing the thread will bend it and prevent it from going through smoothly. Likewise, with relaxation and the right kind of concentration, your internal energy will circulate freely throughout the body, without any blockage.

> **Exercising your internal power is just like refining metal into the purest steel. Then nothing can *not* be destroyed.**

The process of converting internal energy (ch'i) into internal power (jing) requires the meditative exercise of condensing breathing. Then you must learn how to increase and strengthen your internal power through two-person practice.

The growth of your internal power is a gradual process, requiring long periods of exercise, just as the process of refining metal into the purest steel requires constant heat and proper treatment. As a beginner you may have ten percent internal power mixed with ninety percent physical force. Through the constant refining and developing of your internal power, the proportion of physical force will decrease as the amount of internal power available continues to increase. According to Master Wu, when there is pure internal power, pure mind-energy formation, "nothing can *not* be destroyed."

In performing the forms, you should be like the eagle which glides serenely on the wind, but which can swoop instantly to pluck a rabbit from the ground.

When performing the T'ai Chi Meditative Movement, you should allow your internal energy to flow freely so that your forms will be gracefully executed, like the movements of the eagle that glides serenely on the wind. On the other hand, the essence and spirit must be raised, and you must be always ready to "swoop." You should be peaceful yet alert, like the eagle that is able to swoop instantaneously to pluck a rabbit from the ground.

It requires years of practicing the T'ai Chi Meditative Movement in order to achieve this ability.

Your mind should be centered, like the placid cat—peaceful but able to respond instantly to the scurrying mouse.

In order to develop a peaceful and serene state of mind while remaining alert and ready to respond instantly to any change in the environment, the mind should be centered. To achieve this, allow your internal energy to vibrate and extend like the beat of a drum. The spirit must be condensed in toward the center of your body.

When in stillness you should be as the mountain. When in motion you should move like the water of the river.

In T'ai Chi practice you should develop feelings different from those that are normally experienced in daily life. When in stillness, you should feel as if you are a mountain: stable, peaceful, formidable, being yourself. When you are in motion, you should move and feel like the waters of a river: roaring ceaselessly, yielding to any condition, capable of being both peaceful and powerful.

When condensing the internal power, it should be like the pulling of a bow; when projecting the internal power, it should be like the shooting of an arrow.

In the process of converting internal energy into internal power, you must practice condensing breathing techniques in such a way that you feel you are slowly pulling a bow into a fully open position. Projecting the internal power will then be as easy as relaxing your fingertips and letting the arrow go. Any additional effort indicates that a high percentage of physical force is being used.

In T'ai Chi movement, follow the curve to be aware of the straight line. In internal exercise, reserve the energy for transferring the power.

When performing T'ai Chi movements, you should allow your ch'i to drive your body to gracefully follow a curved line; but bear in mind at the same time that the straight line exists.

In internal exercise, especially in condensing breathing, you should constantly practice converting internal energy into internal power. Then accumulate a large amount of jing by storing it.

Transfer of power comes from the spine. Change of position follows the movement of your body.

The transfer of power roots at the foot, travels through the leg, and is controlled by the waist.

The waist serves the same function as the transmission in an automobile: it distributes the amount and direction of your power. After long periods of practice and success in T'ai Chi stance and rooting techniques, the transfer of power will be directly from the waist, following the spine up to the shoulder, and eventually reaching the fingertips. Control of the process of transferring power is therefore located in and mainly depends on your spinal column.

In two-person practice, your stance and steps follow your body movement. In other words, you move your entire body as you change your stance. Changing just your stance or your steps without moving your body will result in loss of control, improper posture, and loss of balance.

Therefore in T'ai Chi "drawing in" leads to "projecting out"; "interruption" leads to "connection."

According to the Yin/Yang theory, the coming of Yang means the coming of Yin. If there is Yang, there is Yin, and vice versa. In practicing the T'ai Chi Movement, therefore, drawing-in motions will automatically lead to projecting-out motions. Interruption of your movement means you are ready to make another connection. When you reach this level of T'ai Chi movement, you will be able to command the art at will.

When you move in and out, your entire body acts like an accordion, folding and unfolding. When you move forward and backward, your stance changes in a varied, dynamic manner.

Because T'ai Chi is based on the Yin/Yang theory of contradiction and balance, when you move forward this means that you are going to move backward. When you move backward, it indicates that you are going to move forward. Each move contains the implication of the opposite direction. When you are moving forward and backward you should relate both movements to each other and act with an accordion-like motion, folding and unfolding.

T'ai Chi philosophy also emphasizes change: Yin must change to Yang and Yang must change to Yin. When you move forward or backward, your stance must change in a dynamic manner.

In T'ai Chi, being very soft and pliable leads to being extremely hard and strong. Command of proper breathing techniques leads to command of free and flexible movement.

In the *Tao-te Ching*, Lao Tzu (ca. 500 B.C.E.) asks, "Can you dedicate your internal energy, ch'i, and be as pliable and yielding as a baby?"

The only condition for allowing your internal energy to develop, grow, and become strong is that you must relax yourself and yield to the universe. When you become soft and pliable, your internal energy will gradually begin to develop and accumulate. Eventually you will have the ability to become extremely hard and strong, when it is necessary to do so. To make metal into the hardest steel, you must heat the metal, make it as soft and pliable as liquid, and then refine it into the hardest steel.

Freedom and flexibility of movement depend on the flow of internal energy. Internal energy development comes from the proper breathing techniques. A beginner in T'ai Chi should therefore examine and develop these techniques.

Cultivate internal energy in a direct way only, and you will do yourself no harm. Store internal power in an indirect way only, and you will build great reserves.

As a T'ai Chi person, you should cultivate your internal energy in daily life. Use any available leisure time to practice your breathing techniques, which will increase your awareness of your internal energy. According to Master Wu, you will never overdo this practice nor cause yourself any harm.

After converting internal energy into internal power, you should also learn how to store this power indirectly. In other words, do not convert internal energy into internal power at the very moment you need it. Instead, save your internal power and reserve it, so that there will be a large amount of power available when needed.

In transferring power, your mind acts like a banner, internal energy acts like a flag, and your waist acts like a pennant. In perfecting your forms, begin with large and extended movements, which, with time, will become compact and concentrated.

In ancient China, army maneuvers were guided by the signals of various-sized flags. The largest banners directed the entire group, the medium-sized flags controlled the various divisions, and the small pennants were used to guide the individual sections. Consequently, the pennant should obey the direction of the flag, which in turn receives orders from the banner. In the same way, transferring power starts from the feet, rises through the legs to the waist, continues up through the back to the shoulders, then through the elbows to the fingers. This all is guided by the mind and controlled at the waist.

The T'ai Chi Meditative Movement includes the high-stance form, the middle-stance form, and the low-stance form, with degrees of extension that can be classified as large, medium, or compact. These can be combined in nine different ways. It is recommended by Master Wu that a beginner start with the large high-stance form, eventually letting the form become more compact and concentrated. Since precise form is required in the beginning, the larger and more extended form will serve better for instruction and correction purposes. After gaining command of the art, you can then discover the same principles in a circular and concentrated form. If instead you begin with compact, concentrated movements, it might not be possible to later perform a large and extended movement correctly.

Also it is said: If there is no motion, you will remain still. If there is even a slight change, you have already moved accordingly.

In two-person practice, relate yourself to your opponent in a Yin/Yang manner. If your opponent offers no motion, you should follow and remain still. If your opponent changes even slightly, you should already be responding accordingly.

T'ai Chi emphasizes the essence of change rather than time, and the essence of relations rather than space. The concept of timing described here refers to pacing, anticipating, and moving ahead of your opponent. It indicates the overlapping of the sequence of changes.

Internal power should remain in a state of equilibrium between relaxed and not-yet-relaxed, extended and not-yet-extended. Even if internal power is interrupted, the mind should remain in continuous action.

T'ai Chi principles stress the meaning of exchange between Yin and Yang. When you exercise your internal power you should remain in a state of being relaxed, but not completely relaxed; extended, but not completely extended.

Even if the internal power is discontinued, there should be a continuation of flow. In two-person practice these principles are very important. You will discover that persons tend to either conflict with each other or not to communicate. This happens because neither of them realizes the true meaning of being relaxed, but not-yet-relaxed; extended, but not-yet-extended. Nor do they understand that the mind should keep the internal power continuously in action.

> Also it is said: First you should exercise your mind, then discipline your body. Relax your abdomen and let internal energy condense into your bone marrow. Make your spirit peaceful and your body calm. Pay attention to your mind at all times.

This is a footnote appended to Master Wu's treatise, which expands basic T'ai Chi principles.

> Bear in mind that once you move, everything should be in motion; when you are still, everything should be in stillness.

Each part of your body should be connected to every other part. Here it is pointed out that when you perform the T'ai Chi Meditative Movement, all parts of your body should be in motion. If you stop any part of your body, the entire body must be stopped.

When practicing Push Hands, as you move forward and backward the internal energy should attach to your back and condense into your spinal column.

This sentence describes the condensing breathing technique and the principle of transferring power as applied to two-person Push Hands practice.

Your spirit should be controlled internally; externally you should appear calm and comfortable.

In Push Hands practice or in martial art application, you must control your spirit and keep it inward. Regardless of how rapidly the situation changes, you should remain calm and easy. This involves mental discipline and indicates that to be a martial artist you should reach the ultimate level of being able to control yourself, in order to cope with any kind of serious situation. Even if a difficult situation builds into a seemingly uncontrollable situation, you should still control yourself in a peaceful and easy manner. Meanwhile, control your spirit internally, allowing no disturbance from any external stimuli.

When changing position, you should move like a cat. Exercising the internal power is like the delicate reeling of silk.

In two-person practice, regardless of which direction you change to, your step must follow the position of your body. In the process of changing steps, you must act and feel like a walking cat—firm and careful.

When controlling or applying your internal power in Push Hands practice, bear in mind that you should maneuver the internal power as if you were reeling silk thread from a cocoon. Reeling too fast will break the silk;

too slow or in the wrong direction may tangle it.

Apply the adequate amount of effort, and apply internal power in the proper direction, with the proper speed.

Your entire body should be controlled by the mind and spirit. Do not attempt to control your body solely by the breathing, because this will make your movements slow and plodding. Controlling the body by breathing yields no internal power; it is only by avoiding such error that you can develop the purest and strongest internal power.

This is a footnote added to explain the relationship between the body and the mind, as well as between internal energy and movement.

Internal power should be likened to the spinning of a wheel. The waist

turns like the axle of a wheel in motion.

Here the analogy indicates that you should keep your internal power in well-balanced and constant motion, like the spinning of a wheel. Your waist controls the amount and distribution of your internal energy, as if it were the axle of a wheel.

LIBRARY OF CONGRESS
CATALOGING-IN-PUBLICATION DATA

Liao, Waysun, 1948–
The essence of T'ai chi/Waysun Liao;
illustrated by the author.—1st ed.
p.   cm—(Shambhala pocket classics)
ISBN 1-57062-039-3 (acid-free paper)
1. T'ai chi ch'üan.
I. Title.   II. Series.
GV504.L527   1994   94-6790
613.7'148—dc20   CIP

(Continued on next page)

(Continued on next page)

THE WAY OF CHUANG TZU
by Thomas Merton

THE WAY OF THE JEWISH MYSTICS
Compiled and edited by Perle Besserman

WAYS OF THE CHRISTIAN MYSTICS
by Thomas Merton

THE WISDOM OF THE DESERT
by Thomas Merton

THE WISDOM OF THE PROPHET
Sayings of Muhammad
Translated by Thomas Cleary

ZEN AND THE BIRDS OF APPETITE
by Thomas Merton

ZEN LESSONS: THE ART OF LEADERSHIP
Translated by Thomas Cleary

THE ZEN TEACHING OF HUANG PO
Translated by John Blofeld

For a complete list, send for our catalogue:

Shambhala Publications
P.O. Box 308
Boston, MA 02117-0308